Terence Rattigan

Born in 1911, a scholar at Harrow and at Trinity College, Oxford,
Terence Rattigan had his first long-running hit in the West End
at the age of twenty-five: *French Without Tears* (1936). His next
play, *After the Dance* (1939), opened to euphoric reviews yet
closed under the gathering clouds of war, but with *Flare Path*
(1942) Rattigan embarked on an almost unbroken series of
successes, with most plays running in the West End for at least a
year and several making the transition to Broadway: *While the Sun
Shines* (1943), *Love in Idleness* (1944), *The Winslow Boy* (1946),
The Browning Version (performed in double-bill with
Harlequinade, 1948), *Who is Sylvia?* (1950), *The Deep Blue Sea*
(1952), *The Sleeping Prince* (1953) and *Separate Tables* (1954).
From the mid-fifties, with the advent of the 'Angry Young Men', he
enjoyed less success on stage, though *Ross* (1960) and *In Praise of
Love* (1973) were well received. As well as seeing many of his
plays turned into successful films, Rattigan wrote a number of
original plays for television from the fifties onwards. He was
knighted in 1971 and died in 1977.

**Other titles by the same author
published by Nick Hern Books**

After the Dance

The Browning Version and *Harlequinade*

Cause Célèbre

The Deep Blue Sea

First Episode

Flare Path

French Without Tears

In Praise of Love

Love in Idleness / Less Than Kind

Rattigan's Nijinsky
    (adapted from Rattigan's screenplay by Nicholas Wright)

Who is Sylvia? and *Duologue*

The Winslow Boy

Terence Rattigan

SEPARATE TABLES

Introduced by
Dan Rebellato

NICK HERN BOOKS
London
www.nickhernbooks.co.uk

A Nick Hern Book

This edition of *Separate Tables* first published
as a paperback original in Great Britain in 1999
by Nick Hern Books, 14 Larden Road, London W3 7ST
by arrangement with Methuen. *Separate Tables* was included
in Volume Three of *The Collected Plays of Terence Rattigan*
published in 1964 by Hamish Hamilton

Reprinted 2009, 2010, 2011

Copyright © Trustees of the Terence Rattigan Trust 1964
Introduction copyright © Dan Rebellato 1999
Front cover photo copyright © Hulton Deutsch Collection

Typeset by Country Setting. Kingsdown, Kent CT14 8ES
Printed and bound by CLE Print Ltd, St Ives, Cambs PE27 3LE

A CIP catalogue record for this book is available from
the British Library

ISBN 978 1 85459 424 2

CAUTION

FSC
www.fsc.org
MIX
From responsible
sources
FSC® C019549

Terence Rattigan (1911-1977)

Terence Rattigan stood on the steps of the Royal Court Theatre,
on 8 May 1956, after the opening night of John Osborne's *Look
Back in Anger*. Asked by a reporter what he thought of the play,
he replied, with an uncharacteristic lack of discretion, that it
should have been retitled 'Look how unlike Terence Rattigan
I'm being.'[1] And he was right. The great shifts in British theatre,
marked by Osborne's famous première, ushered in kinds of
playwriting which were specifically unlike Rattigan's work. The
pre-eminence of playwriting as a formal craft, the subtle tracing
of the emotional lives of the middle classes – those techniques
which Rattigan so perfected – fell dramatically out of favour,
creating a veil of prejudice through which his work even now
struggles to be seen.

Terence Mervyn Rattigan was born on 10 June 1911, a wet Satur-
day a few days before George V's coronation. His father, Frank,
was in the diplomatic corps and Terry's parents were often posted
abroad, leaving him to be raised by his paternal grandmother. Frank
Rattigan was a geographically and emotionally distant man, who
pursued a string of little-disguised affairs throughout his marriage.
Rattigan would later draw on these memories when he created
Mark St Neots, the bourgeois Casanova of *Who is Sylvia?* Rattigan
was much closer to his mother, Vera Rattigan, and they remained
close friends until her death in 1971.

Rattigan's parents were not great theatregoers, but Frank Rattigan's
brother had married a Gaiety Girl, causing a minor family uproar,
and an apocryphal story suggests that the 'indulgent aunt' reported
as taking the young Rattigan to the theatre may have been this
scandalous relation.[2] And when, in the summer of 1922, his family
went to stay in the country cottage of the drama critic Hubert
Griffiths, Rattigan avidly worked through his extensive library of
playscripts. Terry went to Harrow in 1925, and there maintained
both his somewhat illicit theatregoing habit and his insatiable
reading, reputedly devouring every play in the school library. Apart
from contemporary authors like Galsworthy, Shaw and Barrie, he
also read the plays of Chekhov, a writer whose crucial influence he
often acknowledged.[3]

His early attempts at writing, while giving little sign of his later
sophistication, do indicate his ability to absorb and reproduce his
own theatrical experiences. There was a ten-minute melodrama

about the Borgias entitled *The Parchment*, on the cover of which
the author recommends with admirable conviction that a suitable
cast for this work might comprise 'Godfrey Tearle, Gladys Cooper,
Marie Tempest, Matheson Lang, Isobel Elsom, Henry Ainley . . .
[and] Noël Coward'.[4] At Harrow, when one of his teachers
demanded a French playlet for a composition exercise, Rattigan,
undaunted by his linguistic shortcomings, produced a full-throated
tragedy of deception, passion and revenge which included the
immortal curtain line: 'COMTESSE. (*Souffrant terriblement*.) Non!
non! non! Ah non! Mon Dieu, non!'[5] His teacher's now famous
response was 'French execrable: theatre sense first class'.[6] A year
later, aged fifteen, he wrote *The Pure in Heart,* a rather more
substantial play showing a family being pulled apart by a son's
crime and the father's desire to maintain his reputation. Rattigan's
ambitions were plainly indicated on the title pages, each of which
announced the author to be 'the famous playwrite and author T. M.
Rattigan.'[7]

Frank Rattigan was less than keen on having a 'playwrite' for a son
and was greatly relieved when in 1930, paving the way for a life as
a diplomat, Rattigan gained a scholarship to read History at Trinity,
Oxford. But Rattigan's interests were entirely elsewhere. A
burgeoning political conscience that had led him to oppose the
compulsory Officer Training Corps parades at Harrow saw him
voice pacifist and socialist arguments at college, even supporting
the controversial Oxford Union motion 'This House will in no
circumstances fight for its King and Country' in February 1933.
The rise of Hitler (which he briefly saw close at hand when he
spent some weeks in the Black Forest in July 1933) and the
outbreak of the Spanish Civil War saw his radical leanings deepen
and intensify. Rattigan never lost his political compassion. After the
war he drifted towards the Liberal Party, but he always insisted that
he had never voted Conservative, despite the later conception of
him as a Tory playwright of the establishment.[8]

Away from the troubled atmosphere of his family, Rattigan
began to gain in confidence as the contours of his ambitions and
his identity moved more sharply into focus. He soon took
advantage of the university's theatrical facilities and traditions.
He joined The Oxford Union Dramatic Society (OUDS), where
contemporaries included Giles Playfair, George Devine, Peter
Glenville, Angus Wilson and Frith Banbury. Each year, OUDS ran
a one-act play competition and in Autumn 1931 Rattigan
submitted one. Unusually, it seems that this was a highly experi-
mental effort, somewhat like Konstantin's piece in *The Seagull*.
George Devine, the OUDS president, apparently told the young
author, 'Some of it is absolutely smashing, but it goes too far'.[9]
Rattigan was instead to make his first mark as a somewhat
scornful reviewer for the student newspaper, *Cherwell*, and as a

performer in the Smokers (OUDS's private revue club), where he adopted the persona and dress of 'Lady Diana Coutigan', a drag performance which allowed him to discuss leading members of the Society with a barbed camp wit.[10]

That the name of his Smokers persona echoed the contemporary phrase, 'queer as a coot', indicates Rattigan's new-found confidence in his homosexuality. In February 1932, Rattigan played a tiny part in the OUDS production of *Romeo and Juliet*, which was directed by John Gielgud and starred Peggy Ashcroft and Edith Evans (women undergraduates were not admitted to OUDS, and professional actresses were often recruited). Rattigan's failure to deliver his one line correctly raised an increasingly embarrassing laugh every night (an episode which he re-uses to great effect in *Harlequinade*). However, out of this production came a friendship with Gielgud and his partner, John Perry. Through them, Rattigan was introduced to theatrical and homosexual circles, where his youthful 'school captain' looks were much admired.

A growing confidence in his sexuality and in his writing led to his first major play. In 1931, he shared rooms with a contemporary of his, Philip Heimann, who was having an affair with Irina Basilevich, a mature student. Rattigan's own feelings for Heimann completed an eternal triangle that formed the basis of the play he co-wrote with Heimann, *First Episode*. This play was accepted for production in Surrey's "Q" theatre; it was respectfully received and subsequently transferred to the Comedy Theatre in London's West End, though carefully shorn of its homosexual subplot. Despite receiving only £50 from this production (and having put £200 into it), Rattigan immediately dropped out of college to become a full-time writer.

Frank Rattigan was displeased by this move, but made a deal with his son. He would give him an allowance of £200 a year for two years and let him live at home to write; if at the end of that period, he had had no discernible success, he would enter a more secure and respectable profession. With this looming deadline, Rattigan wrote quickly. *Black Forest*, an O'Neill-inspired play based on his experiences in Germany in 1933, is one of the three that have survived. Rather unwillingly, he collaborated with Hector Bolitho on an adaptation of the latter's novel, *Grey Farm*, which received a disastrous New York production in 1940. Another project was an adaptation of *A Tale of Two Cities*, written with Gielgud; this fell through at the last minute when Donald Albery, the play's potential producer, received a complaint from actor-manager John Martin-Harvey who was beginning a farewell tour of his own adaptation, *The Only Way*, which he had been performing for forty-five years. As minor compensation, Albery invited Rattigan to send him any other new scripts. Rattigan sent him a play provisionally titled *Gone Away*, based on his experiences in a French language Summer School in 1931. Albery took out a nine-month option on it, but no production appeared.

By mid-1936, Rattigan was despairing. His father had secured him a job with Warner Brothers as an in-house screenwriter, which was reasonably paid; but Rattigan wanted success in the theatre, and his desk-bound life at Teddington Studios seemed unlikely to advance this ambition. By chance, one of Albery's productions was unexpectedly losing money, and the wisest course of action seemed to be to pull the show and replace it with something cheap. Since *Gone Away* required a relatively small cast and only one set, Albery quickly arranged for a production. Harold French, the play's director, had only one qualm: the title. Rattigan suggested *French Without Tears*, which was immediately adopted.

After an appalling dress rehearsal, no one anticipated the rapturous response of the first-night audience, led by Cicely Courtneidge's infectious laugh. The following morning Kay Hammond, the show's female lead, discovered Rattigan surrounded by the next day's reviews. 'But I don't believe it', he said. 'Even *The Times* likes it.' [11]

French Without Tears played over 1000 performances in its three-year run and Rattigan was soon earning £100 a week. He moved out of his father's home, wriggled out of his Warner Brothers contract, and dedicated himself to spending the money as soon as it came in. Partly this was an attempt to defer the moment when he had to follow up this enormous success. In the event, both of his next plays were undermined by the outbreak of war.

After the Dance, an altogether more bleak indictment of the Bright Young Things' failure to engage with the iniquities and miseries of contemporary life, opened, in June 1939, to euphoric reviews; but only a month later the European crisis was darkening the national mood and audiences began to dwindle. The play was pulled in August after only sixty performances. *Follow My Leader* was a satirical farce closely based on the rise of Hitler, co-written with an Oxford contemporary, Tony Goldschmidt (writing as Anthony Maurice in case anyone thought he was German). It suffered an alternative fate. Banned from production in 1938, owing to the Foreign Office's belief that 'the production of this play at this time would not be in the best interests of the country',[12] it finally received its première in 1940, by which time Rattigan and Goldschmidt's mild satire failed to capture the real fears that the war was unleashing in the country.

Rattigan's insecurity about writing now deepened. An interest in Freud, dating back to his Harrow days, encouraged him to visit a psychiatrist that he had known while at Oxford, Dr Keith Newman. Newman exerted a svengali-like influence on Rattigan and persuaded the pacifist playwright to join the RAF as a means of curing his writer's block. Oddly, this unorthodox treatment seemed to have some effect; by 1941, Rattigan was writing again. On one dramatic sea crossing, an engine failed, and with everyone forced to jettison all excess baggage and possessions, Rattigan threw the hard covers and blank pages from the notebook containing his new play, stuffing the precious manuscript into his jacket.

Rattigan drew on his RAF experiences to write a new play, *Flare Path*. Bronson Albery and Bill Linnit who had both supported *French Without Tears* both turned the play down, believing that the last thing that the public wanted was a play about the war.[13] H. M. Tennent Ltd., led by the elegant Hugh 'Binkie' Beaumont, was the third management offered the script; and in 1942, *Flare Path* opened in London, eventually playing almost 700 performances. Meticulously interweaving the stories of three couples against the backdrop of wartime uncertainty, Rattigan found himself 'commended, if not exactly as a professional playwright, at least as a promising apprentice who had definitely begun to learn the rudiments of his job'.[14] Beaumont, already on the way to becoming the most powerful and successful West End producer of the era, was an influential ally for Rattigan. There is a curious side-story to this production; Dr Keith Newman decided to watch 250 performances of this play and write up the insights that his 'serial attendance' had afforded him. George Bernard Shaw remarked that such playgoing behaviour 'would have driven me mad; and I am not sure that [Newman] came out of it without a slight derangement'. Shaw's caution was wise.[15] In late 1945, Newman went insane and eventually died in a psychiatric hospital.

Meanwhile, Rattigan had achieved two more successes; the witty farce, *While the Sun Shines*, and the more serious, though politically clumsy, *Love in Idleness* (retitled *O Mistress Mine* in America). He had also co-written a number of successful films, including *The Day Will Dawn, Uncensored, The Way to the Stars* and an adaptation of *French Without Tears*. By the end of 1944, Rattigan had three plays running in the West End, a record only beaten by Somerset Maugham's four in 1908.

Love in Idleness was dedicated to Henry 'Chips' Channon, the Tory MP who had become Rattigan's lover. Channon's otherwise gossipy diaries record their meeting very discreetly: 'I dined with Juliet Duff in her little flat . . . also there, Sibyl Colefax and Master Terence Rattigan, and we sparkled over the Burgundy. I like Rattigan enormously, and feel a new friendship has begun. He has a flat in Albany'.[16] Tom Driberg's rather less discreet account fleshes out the story: Channon's 'seduction of the playwright was almost like the wooing of Danaë by Zeus – every day the playwright found, delivered to his door, a splendid present – a case of champagne, a

huge pot of caviar, a Cartier cigarette-box in two kinds of gold . . .
In the end, of course, he gave in, saying apologetically to his
friends, "How can one *not?*" '.[17] It was a very different set in which
Rattigan now moved, one that was wealthy and conservative, the
very people he had criticised in *After the Dance*. Rattigan did not
share the complacency of many of his friends, and his next play
revealed a deepening complexity and ambition.

For a long time, Rattigan had nurtured a desire to become respected
as a serious writer; the commercial success of *French Without
Tears* had, however, sustained the public image of Rattigan as a
wealthy young light comedy writer-about-town. [18] With *The
Winslow Boy*, which premièred in 1946, Rattigan began to turn this
image around. In doing so he entered a new phase as a playwright.
As one contemporary critic observed, this play 'put him at once
into the class of the serious and distinguished writer'.[19] The play,
based on the Archer-Shee case in which a family attempted to sue
the Admiralty for a false accusation of theft against their son,
featured some of Rattigan's most elegantly crafted and subtle
characterization yet. The famous second curtain, when the barrister
Robert Morton subjects Ronnie Winslow to a vicious interrogation
before announcing that 'The boy is plainly innocent. I accept the
brief', brought a joyous standing ovation on the first night. No less
impressive is the subtle handling of the concept of 'justice' and
'rights' through the play of ironies which pits Morton's liberal
complacency against Catherine Winslow's feminist convictions.

Two years later, Rattigan's *Playbill*, comprising the one-act plays
The Browning Version and *Harlequinade*, showed an ever
deepening talent. The latter is a witty satire of the kind of touring
theatre encouraged by the new Committee for the Encouragement
of Music and Arts (CEMA, the immediate forerunner of the Arts
Council). But the former's depiction of a failed, repressed Classics
teacher evinced an ability to choreograph emotional subtleties on
stage that outstripped anything Rattigan had yet demonstrated.

Adventure Story, which in 1949 followed hard on the heels of
Playbill, was less successful. An attempt to dramatize the emotional
dilemmas of Alexander the Great, Rattigan seemed unable to escape
the vernacular of his own circle, and the epic scheme of the play sat
oddly with Alexander's more prosaic concerns.

Rattigan's response to both the critical bludgeoning of this play and
the distinctly luke-warm reception of *Playbill* on Broadway was to
write a somewhat extravagant article for the *New Statesman*.
'Concerning the Play of Ideas' was a desire to defend the place of
'character' against those who would insist on the pre-eminence in
drama of ideas.[20] The essay is not clear and is couched in such
teasing terms that it is at first difficult to see why it should have
secured such a fervent response. James Bridie, Benn Levy, Peter

Ustinov, Sean O'Casey, Ted Willis, Christopher Fry and finally George Bernard Shaw all weighed in to support or condemn the article. Finally Rattigan replied in slightly more moderate terms to these criticisms insisting (and the first essay reasonably supports this) that he was not calling for the end of ideas in the theatre, but rather for their inflection through character and situation.[21] However, the damage was done (as, two years later, with his 'Aunt Edna', it would again be done). Rattigan was increasingly being seen as the arch-proponent of commercial vacuity.[22]

The play Rattigan had running at the time added weight to his opponents' charge. Originally planned as a dark comedy, *Who is Sylvia?* became a rather more frivolous thing both in the writing and the playing. Rattled by the failure of *Adventure Story*, and superstitiously aware that the new play was opening at the Criterion, where fourteen years before *French Without Tears* had been so successful, Rattigan and everyone involved in the production had steered it towards light farce and obliterated the residual seriousness of the original conceit.

Rattigan had ended his affair with Henry Channon and taken up with Kenneth Morgan, a young actor who had appeared in *Follow My Leader* and the film of *French Without Tears*. However, the relationship had not lasted and Morgan had for a while been seeing someone else. Rattigan's distress was compounded one day in February 1949, when he received a message that Morgan had killed himself. Although horrified, Rattigan soon began to conceive an idea for a play. Initially it was to have concerned a homosexual relationship, but Beaumont, his producer, persuaded him to change the relationship to a heterosexual one.[23] At a time when the Lord Chamberlain refused to allow any plays to be staged that featured homosexuality, such a proposition would have been a commercial impossibility. The result is one of the finest examples of Rattigan's craft. The story of Hester Collyer, trapped in a relationship with a man incapable of returning her love, and her transition from attempted suicide to groping, uncertain self-determination is handled with extraordinary economy, precision and power. The depths of despair and desire that Rattigan plumbs have made *The Deep Blue Sea* one of his most popular and moving pieces.

1953 saw Rattigan's romantic comedy *The Sleeping Prince*, planned as a modest, if belated, contribution to the Coronation festivities. However, the project was hypertrophied by the insistent presence of Laurence Olivier and Vivien Leigh in the cast and the critics were disturbed to see such whimsy from the author of *The Deep Blue Sea*.

Two weeks after its opening, the first two volumes of Rattigan's *Collected Plays* were published. The preface to the second volume introduced one of Rattigan's best-known, and most notorious creations: Aunt Edna. 'Let us invent,' he writes, 'a character, a

nice respectable, middle-class, middle-aged, maiden lady, with
time on her hands and the money to help her pass it'.[24] Rattigan
paints a picture of this eternal theatregoer, whose bewildered
disdain for modernism ('Picasso—"those dreadful reds, my dear,
and why three noses?" ')[25] make up part of the particular challenge
of dramatic writing. The intertwined commercial and cultural
pressures that the audience brings with it exert considerable force
on the playwright's work.

Rattigan's creation brought considerable scorn upon his head. But
Rattigan is neither patronizing nor genuflecting towards Aunt
Edna. The whole essay is aimed at demonstrating the crucial rôle
of the audience in the theatrical experience. Rattigan's own sense
of theatre was *learned* as a member of the audience, and he
refuses to distance himself from this woman: 'despite my already
self-acknowledged creative ambitions I did not in the least feel
myself a being apart. If my neighbours gasped with fear for the
heroine when she was confronted with a fate worse than death, I
gasped with them'.[26] But equally, he sees his job as a writer to
engage in a gentle tug-of-war with the audience's expectations:
'although Aunt Edna must never be made mock of, or bored, or
befuddled, she must equally not be wooed, or pandered to or
cosseted'.[27] The complicated relation between satisfying and
surprising this figure may seem contradictory, but as Rattigan
notes, 'Aunt Edna herself is indeed a highly contradictory
character'.[28]

But Rattigan's argument, as in the 'Play of Ideas' debate before it,
was taken to imply an insipid pandering to the unchallenging
expectations of his audience. Aunt Edna dogged his career from
that moment on and she became such a by-word for what theatre
should *not* be that in 1960, the Questors Theatre, Ealing, could title
a triple-bill of Absurdist plays, 'Not For Aunt Edna'.[29]

Rattigan's next play did help to restore his reputation as a serious
dramatist. *Separate Tables* was another double-bill, set in a small
Bournemouth hotel. The first play develops Rattigan's familiar
themes of sexual longing and humiliation while the second pits a
man found guilty of interfering with women in a local cinema
against the self-appointed moral jurors in the hotel. The evening
was highly acclaimed and the subsequent Broadway production a
rare American success.

However, Rattigan's reign as the leading British playwright was
about to be brought to an abrupt end. In a car from Stratford to
London, early in 1956, Rattigan spent two and a half hours
informing his Oxford contemporary George Devine why the new
play he had discovered would not work in the theatre. When
Devine persisted, Rattigan answered 'Then I know nothing about
plays'. To which Devine replied, 'You know everything about

plays, but you don't know a fucking thing about *Look Back in Anger*.' [30] Rattigan only barely attended the first night. He and Hugh Beaumont wanted to leave at the interval until the critic T. C. Worsley persuaded them to stay.[31]

The support for the English Stage Company's initiative was soon overwhelming. Osborne's play was acclaimed by the influential critics Kenneth Tynan and Harold Hobson, and the production was revived frequently at the Court, soon standing as the banner under which that disparate band of men (and women), the Angry Young Men, would assemble. Like many of his contemporaries, Rattigan decried the new movements, Beckett and Ionesco's turn from Naturalism, the wild invective of Osborne, the passionate socialism of Wesker, the increasing influence of Brecht. His opposition to them was perhaps intemperate, but he knew what was at stake: 'I may be prejudiced, but I'm pretty sure it won't survive,' he said in 1960, 'I'm prejudiced because if it *does* survive, I know I won't.' [32]

Such was the power and influence of the new movement that Rattigan almost immediately seemed old-fashioned. And from now on, his plays began to receive an almost automatic panning. His first play since *Separate Tables* (1954) was *Variation on a Theme* (1958). But between those dates the critical mood had changed. To make matters worse, there was the widely publicized story that nineteen year-old Shelagh Delaney had written the successful *A Taste of Honey* in two weeks after having seen *Variation on a Theme* and deciding that she could do better. A more sinister aspect of the response was the increasingly open accusation that Rattigan was dishonestly concealing a covert homosexual play within an apparently heterosexual one. The two champions of Osborne's play, Tynan and Hobson, were joined by Gerard Fay in the *Manchester Guardian* and Alan Brien in the *Spectator* to ask 'Are Things What They Seem?' [33]

When he is not being attacked for smuggling furtively homosexual themes into apparently straight plays, Rattigan is also criticized for lacking the courage to 'come clean' about his sexuality, both in his life and in his writing.[34] But neither of these criticisms really hit the mark. On the one hand, it is rather disingenuous to suggest that Rattigan should have 'come out'. The 1950s were a difficult time for homosexual men. The flight to the Soviet Union of Burgess and Maclean in 1951 sparked off a major witch-hunt against homosexuals, especially those in prominent positions. Cecil Beaton and Benjamin Britten were rumoured to be targets.[35] The police greatly stepped up the investigation and entrapment of homosexuals and prosecutions rose dramatically at the end of the forties, reaching a peak in 1953-54. One of their most infamous arrests for importuning, in October 1953, was that of John Gielgud.[36]

But neither is it quite correct to imply that somehow Rattigan's plays are *really* homosexual. This would be to misunderstand the way that homosexuality figured in the forties and early fifties. Wartime London saw a considerable expansion in the number of pubs and bars where homosexual men (and women) could meet. This network sustained a highly sophisticated system of gestural and dress codes, words and phrases that could be used to indicate one's sexual desires, many of them drawn from theatrical slang. But the illegality of any homosexual activity ensured that these codes could never become *too* explicit, *too* clear. Homosexuality, then, was explored and experienced through a series of semi-hidden, semi-open codes of behaviour; the image of the iceberg, with the greater part of its bulk submerged beneath the surface, was frequently employed.[37] And this image is, of course, one of the metaphors often used to describe Rattigan's own playwriting.

Reaction came in the form of a widespread paranoia about the apparent increase in homosexuality. The fifties saw a major drive to seek out, understand, and often 'cure' homosexuality. The impetus of these investigations was to bring the unspeakable and underground activities of, famously, 'Evil Men' into the open, to make it fully visible. The Wolfenden Report of 1957 was, without doubt, a certain kind of liberalizing document in its recommendation that consensual sex between adult men in private be legalized. However the other side of its effect is to reinstate the integrity of those boundaries – private/public, hidden/exposed, homosexual/heterosexual – which homosexuality was broaching. The criticisms of Rattigan are precisely part of this same desire to divide, clarify and expose.

Many of Rattigan's plays were originally written with explicit homosexual characters (*French Without Tears*, *The Deep Blue Sea* and *Separate Tables*, for example), which he then changed.[38] But many more of them hint at homosexual experiences and activities: the relationship between Tony and David in *First Episode*, the Major in *Follow my Leader* who is blackmailed over an incident in Baghdad ('After all,' he explains, 'a chap's only human, and it was a deuced hot night –'),[39] the suspiciously polymorphous servicemen of *While the Sun Shines*, Alexander the Great and T. E. Lawrence from *Adventure Story* and *Ross*, Mr Miller in *The Deep Blue Sea* and several others. Furthermore, rumours of Rattigan's own bachelor life circulated fairly widely. As indicated above, Rattigan always placed great trust in the audiences of his plays, and it was the audience which had to decode and reinterpret these plays. His plays cannot be judged by the criterion of 'honesty' and 'explicitness' that obsessed a generation after Osborne. They are plays which negotiate sexual desire through structures of hint, implications and metaphor. As David Rudkin has suggested, 'the craftsmanship of which we hear so much loose

talk seems to me to arise from deep psychological necessity, a
drive to organize the energy that arises out of his own pain. Not to
batten it down but to invest it with some expressive clarity that
speaks immediately to people, yet keeps itself hidden'.[40]

The shifts in the dominant view of both homosexuality and
the theatre that took place in the fifties account for the brutal
decline of Rattigan's career. He continued writing, and while
Ross (1960) was reasonably well received, his ill-judged musical
adaptation of *French Without Tears*, *Joie de Vivre* (1960), was
a complete disaster, not assisted by a liberal bout of laryngitis
among the cast, and the unexpected insanity of the pianist.[41] It
ran for four performances.

During the sixties, Rattigan was himself dogged with ill-health:
pneumonia and hepatitis were followed by leukaemia. When his
death conspicuously failed to transpire, this last diagnosis was
admitted to be incorrect. Despite this, he continued to write,
producing the successful television play *Heart to Heart* in 1962,
and the stage play *Man and Boy* the following year, which received
the same sniping that greeted *Variation on a Theme*. In 1964, he
wrote *Nelson – a Portrait in Miniature* for Associated Television,
as part of a short season of his plays.

It was at this point that Rattigan decided to leave Britain and live
abroad. Partly this decision was taken for reasons of health; but
partly Rattigan just seemed no longer to be welcome. Ironically, it
was the same charge being levelled at Rattigan that he had faced in
the thirties, when the newspapers thundered against the those who
had supported the Oxford Union's pacifist motion as 'woolly-
minded Communists, practical jokers and sexual indeterminates'.[42]
As he confessed in an interview late in his life, 'Overnight almost,
we were told we were old-fashioned and effete and corrupt and
finished, and . . . I somehow accepted Tynan's verdict and went off
to Hollywood to write film scripts'.[43] In 1967 he moved to
Bermuda as a tax exile. A stage adaptation of his Nelson play, as
Bequest to the Nation, had a luke-warm reception.

Rattigan had a bad sixties, but his seventies seemed to indicate a
turnaround in his fortunes and reputation. At the end of 1970, a
successful production of *The Winslow Boy* was the first of ten
years of acclaimed revivals. In 1972, Hampstead Theatre revived
While the Sun Shines and a year later the Young Vic was praised
for its *French Without Tears*. In 1976 and 1977 *The Browning
Version* was revived at the King's Head and *Separate Tables* at
the Apollo. Rattigan briefly returned to Britain in 1971, pulled
partly by his renewed fortune and partly by the fact that he was
given a knighthood in the New Year's honours list. Another double
bill followed in 1973: *In Praise of Love* comprised the weak
Before Dawn and the moving tale of emotional concealment and

creativity, *After Lydia*. Critical reception was more respectful than usual, although the throwaway farce of the first play detracted from the quality of the second.

Cause Célèbre, commissioned by BBC Radio and others, concerned the Rattenbury case, in which Alma Rattenbury's aged husband was beaten to death by her eighteen year-old lover. Shortly after its radio première, Rattigan was diagnosed with bone cancer. Rattigan's response, having been through the false leukaemia scare in the early sixties, was to greet the news with unruffled elegance, welcoming the opportunity to 'work harder and indulge myself more'.[44] The hard work included a play about the Asquith family and a stage adaptation of *Cause Célèbre*, but, as production difficulties began to arise over the latter, the Asquith play slipped out of Rattigan's grasp. Although very ill, he returned to Britain, and on 4 July 1977, he was taken by limousine from his hospital bed to Her Majesty's Theatre, where he watched his last ever première. A fortnight later he had a car drive him around the West End where two of his plays were then running before boarding the plane for the last time. On 30 November 1977, in Bermuda, he died.

As Michael Billington's perceptive obituary noted, 'his whole work is a sustained assault on English middle class values: fear of emotional commitment, terror in the face of passion, apprehension about sex'.[45] In death, Rattigan began once again to be seen as someone critically opposed to the values with which he had so long been associated, a writer dramatizing dark moments of bleak compassion and aching desire.

Notes.

1. Quoted in Rattigan's *Daily Telegraph* obituary (1 December 1977).

2. Michael Darlow and Gillian Hodson. *Terence Rattigan: The Man and His Work*. London and New York: Quartet Books, 1979, p. 26.

3. See, for example, Sheridan Morley. 'Terence Rattigan at 65.' *The Times*. (9 May 1977).

4. Terence Rattigan. Preface. *The Collected Plays of Terence Rattigan: Volume Two*. London: Hamish Hamilton, 1953, p. xv.

5. *Ibid.,* p. viii.

6. *Ibid.,* p. vii.

7. *Ibid.,* p. vii.

8. cf. Sheridan Morley, *op. cit.*

9. Humphrey Carpenter. *OUDS: A Centenary History of the Oxford University Dramatic Society*. With a Prologue by Robert Robinson. Oxford: Oxford University Press, 1985, p. 123.

10. Rattigan may well have reprised this later in life. John Osborne, in his autobiography, recalls a friend showing him a picture of Rattigan performing in an RAF drag show: 'He showed me a photograph of himself with Rattigan, dressed in a *tutu*, carrying a wand, accompanied by a line of aircraftsmen, during which Terry had sung his own show-stopper, "I'm just about the oldest fairy in the business. I'm quite the oldest fairy that you've ever seen".' John

Osborne. *A Better Class of Person: An Autobiography, Volume I 1929-1956*. London: Faber and Faber, 1981, p. 223.

11. Darlow and Hodson *op. cit.*, p. 83.

12. Norman Gwatkin. Letter to Gilbert Miller, 28 July 1938. in: *Follow My Leader*. Lord Chamberlain's Correspondence: LR 1938. [British Library].

13. Richard Huggett. *Binkie Beaumont: Eminence Grise of the West Theatre 1933-1973*. London: Hodder & Stoughton, 1989, p. 308.

14. Terence Rattigan. Preface. *The Collected Plays of Terence Rattigan: Volume One*. London: Hamish Hamilton, 1953, p. xiv.

15. George Bernard Shaw, in: Keith Newman. *Two Hundred and Fifty Times I Saw a Play: or, Authors, Actors and Audiences*. With the facsimile of a comment by Bernard Shaw. Oxford: Pelagos Press, 1944, p. 2.

16. Henry Channon. *Chips: The Diaries of Sir Henry Channon*. Edited by Robert Rhodes James. Harmondsworth: Penguin, 1974, p. 480. Entry for 29 September 1944.

17. Tom Driberg. *Ruling Passions*. London: Jonathan Cape, 1977, p. 186.

18. See, for example, Norman Hart. 'Introducing Terence Rattigan,' *Theatre World*. xxxi, 171. (April 1939). p. 180 or Ruth Jordan. 'Another Adventure Story,' *Woman's Journal*. (August 1949), pp. 31-32.

19. Audrey Williamson. *Theatre of Two Decades*. New York and London: Macmillan, 1951, p. 100.

20. Terence Rattigan. 'Concerning the Play of Ideas,' *New Statesman and Nation*. (4 March 1950), pp. 241-242.

21. Terence Rattigan. 'The Play of Ideas,' *New Statesman and Nation*. (13 May 1950), pp. 545-546. See also Susan Rusinko, 'Rattigan versus Shaw: The 'Drama of Ideas' Debate'. in: *Shaw: The Annual of Bernard Shaw Studies: Volume Two*. Edited by Stanley Weintraub. University Park, Penn: Pennsylvania State University Press, 1982. pp. 171-78.

22. John Elsom writes that Rattigan's plays 'represented establishment writing'. *Post-War British Drama*. Revised Edition. London: Routledge, 1979, p. 33.

23. B. A. Young. *The Rattigan Version: Sir Terence Rattigan and the Theatre of Character*. Hamish Hamilton: London, 1986, pp. 102-103; and Darlow and Hodson, *op. cit.*, p. 196, 204n.

24. Terence Rattigan. *Coll. Plays: Vol. Two. op. cit.*, pp. xi-xii.

25. *Ibid.*, p. xii.

26. *Ibid.*, p. xiv.

27. *Ibid.*, p. xvi.

28. *Ibid.*, p. xviii.

29. Opened on 17 September 1960. cf. *Plays and Players*. vii, 11 (November 1960).

30. Quoted in Irving Wardle. *The Theatres of George Devine*. London: Jonathan Cape, 1978, p. 180.

31. John Osborne. *Almost a Gentleman: An Autobiography, Volume II 1955-1966*. London: Faber and Faber, 1991, p. 20.

32. Robert Muller. 'Soul-Searching with Terence Rattigan.' *Daily Mail*. (30 April 1960).

33. The headline of Hobson's review in the *Sunday Times*, 11 May 1958.

34. See, for example, Nicholas de Jongh. *Not in Front of the Audience: Homosexuality on Stage*. London: Routledge, 1992, pp. 55-58.

35. Kathleen Tynan. *The Life of Kenneth Tynan*. Corrected Edition. London: Methuen, 1988, p. 118.

36. Cf. Jeffrey Weeks. *Coming Out: Homosexual Politics in Britain from the Nineteenth Century to the Present*. Revised and Updated Edition. London and New York: Quartet, 1990, p. 58; Peter Wildeblood. *Against the Law*.

London: Weidenfeld and Nicolson, 1955, p. 46. The story of Gielgud's arrest may be found in Huggett, *op. cit.,* pp. 429-431. It was Gielgud's arrest which apparently inspired Rattigan to write the second part of *Separate Tables*, although again, thanks this time to the Lord Chamberlain, Rattigan had to change the Major's offence to a heterosexual one. See Darlow and Hodson, *op. cit.*, p. 228.

37. See, for example, Rodney Garland's novel about homosexual life in London, *The Heart in Exile*. London: W. H. Allen, 1953, p. 104.

38. See note 36; and also 'Rattigan Talks to John Simon,' *Theatre Arts*. 46 (April 1962), p. 24.

39. Terence Rattigan and Anthony Maurice. *Follow my Leader.* Typescript. Lord Chamberlain Play Collection: 1940/2. Box 2506. [British Library].

40. Quoted in Darlow and Hodson, *op. cit.,* p. 15.

41. B. A. Young, *op. cit.,* p. 162.

42. Quoted in Darlow and Hodson, *op. cit.,* p. 56.

43. Quoted in Sheridan Morley, *op. cit.*

44. Darlow and Hodson, *op. cit.,* p. 308.

45. *Guardian.* (2 December 1977).

Separate Tables

In November 1956, towards the end of the two-year run of
Separate Tables in the West End, Terence Rattigan was at the
height of his career. After playing to full houses and overwhelm-
ingly approving reviews in London, the play had just opened
in New York to be hailed as the first triumphant success of the
1956/57 Broadway season. *The Sleeping Prince,* his *pièce
d'occasion*, written to mark Elizabeth II's coronation, was being
filmed with Laurence Olivier and Marilyn Monroe. The cinema
rights to *Separate Tables* had been sold, and the resulting film
would eventually accrue Oscar nominations in seven categories,
and win in two of them.

But over the previous six months, things had been stirring in
British theatre. John Osborne's *Look Back in Anger,* which
Rattigan had dismissed intemperately at its premiere in May 1956,
marked the beginning of a sea-change in theatrical tastes; the
names of Osborne, Wesker, Delaney, and Pinter would, by the end
of the decade, have eclipsed the names of Coward, Priestley, Eliot
and Fry. The sharp realignment of allegiances was firmly brought
home to Rattigan in 1958 in the barrage of scornful, dismissive
reviews that greeted his next play, *Variation on a Theme*. Despite
producing powerful and challenging work in the sixties and
seventies like *Ross, Man and Boy, In Praise of Love* and *Cause
Célèbre,* Rattigan was now treated as a stilted curiosity from a
happily forgotten era. *Separate Tables* was his last success before
perhaps the most sudden and dramatic fall from grace of any
playwright this century.

However, this picture is inevitably somewhat oversimplified.
Throughout the fifties, there had been growing debate about his
work, and what he stood for. *Separate Tables* has historically
carried the burden of competing views of Rattigan, which are still
at play in the contemporary response to this piece.

For Rattigan, the decade had begun with his article 'Concerning the
Play of Ideas' in *The New Statesman and Nation*. Rattigan often
overreached himself when making programmatic statements about
the theatre, and nowhere more than here, in his simplistic
declaration that 'From Aeschylus to Tennessee Williams the only
theatre that has ever mattered is the theatre of character and
narrative' and that 'ideas . . . take third place'.[1] There is something
of a contradiction between denouncing ideas in the theatre and

propounding them in the *New Statesman*, and his statement, in any case, underestimated the way in which his own plays often artfully depict social forces *through* character and narrative. His article unleashed the combined assault of, amongst others, James Bridie, Sean O'Casey, Ted Willis, Christopher Fry and eventually George Bernard Shaw, choosing to set this 'irrational genius' right in a dazzling, if opaque, outline of the role of ideas in theatrical history.[2] Rattigan's final response, claiming masochistically to be honoured by the calibre of caning he had received, shows some recognition of the flaws in his initial conception, particularly in his admission that perhaps his rating of character above ideas was a 'question of emphasis' rather than a categorical exclusion of the latter by the former.[3]

Nonetheless, Rattigan returned to the fray in 1953 when the first two volumes of his *Collected Plays* were published. In his introduction to the second volume, Rattigan is musing on his desire to become a playwright. Even, when youthfully trying his hand at prose, he notes, his real ambitions were clear from the grandiose title page which proudly announced the work to be 'an enthralling novelette by the famous [...] playwrite and author...'.[4] The precedence of 'playwrite' over author indicated a preference for writing which would be tested against an audience, and Rattigan insisted that this audience, in all its contradictions, is a crucial element in the formulation and construction of a play.

Rattigan was not exactly his own worst enemy, but he could be one of them. It was evidently a feeling of the greatest self-confidence, and perhaps of scores left unsettled from the 'Play of Ideas' controversy, that impelled him to invent Aunt Edna (see biographical introduction, pp. xi-xii). This characterisation of the contemporary theatre audience as a middle-class, middle-aged, middle-brow housewife was not, as I have argued elsewhere, an unreasonable, nor wholly uncomplicated, invention;[5] yet Edna was seized upon (and his reception at the *New Statesman* might have prepared him for this) as a projection of Rattigan's supposedly complacent and timid theatrical ambitions. Joe Orton's later, satirical invention of Edna Welthorpe, the permanently scandalised crusader for Middle England, is a clear echo of Rattigan's creation.[6]

Separate Tables, Rattigan's first major play to open in Edna's wake, had its reception muted by the hesitation she was occasioning in the minds of his critics. The play was well reviewed; Maurice Wiltshire, in the *Daily Mail*, declared that 'the high point reached by Mr Rattigan as a serious dramatist in *The Deep Blue Sea* has been passed. In my opinion he is now without question the master playwright of our day'.[7] But a recurring ploy of the reviewers is to pay a backhanded compliment to Rattigan's ability as a craftsman and a storyteller. W. A. Darlington admitted he was not moved by the play, yet praised the way that 'all the skill that had gone into its making [is] cunningly concealed'. Anthony Cookman praises Rattigan's 'skill' in a review for *The Tatler and Bystander* which was headlined 'Craftsman at Work'. J. C. Trewin refers to Rattigan as 'professional' six times across his reviews for the *Illustrated London News* and *The Sketch*. In the former he writes, 'it does not spring from life. It is Mr Rattigan inventing a good story'.

What underlies these attacks of faint praise is a worry that Rattigan's 'professional skill' is that of a manipulator, whose real feelings are softened by his desire to please Aunt Edna. The reviewer in *The Times* comes out with it, as he amplifies the widespread uncertainty by saying that, in *Separate Tables*, Rattigan is 'almost at his best as an artist and quite at his best as a storyteller who is careful to please the numerous body of playgoers whom he has personified in an Aunt Edna'. The reviewer goes on: 'His Aunt Edna [...] likes happy endings and she is not over particular as to the dramatic methods employed to bring them about. Mr Rattigan's determination to consult her wishes on this matter doubtless accounts for a faint streak of falsity which runs through these extremely interesting stage stories'. Milton Shulman in the *Evening Standard* and John Barber in the *Daily Express* both detect the same feigned quality, Barber claiming that 'in both plays you see the exact point at which Rattigan stops telling the truth about his people'. Kenneth Tynan's review took the form of a dialogue between Aunt Edna and a Young Perfectionist, ending with the brilliantly damning exchange:

AUNT EDNA. Clearly, there is something here for both of us.
YOUNG PERFECTIONIST. Yes. But not quite enough for either of us.[8]

This sense of Rattigan being caught between the incompatible demands of theatre's young idealists and its hidebound Ednas would be fully articulated and nailed to Rattigan's reputation after 1956. It is, indeed, a charge that has been laid against many of the playwrights of Rattigan's generation; plays like J. B. Priestley's *An Inspector Calls* were for a long time dismissed as repertory-theatre warhorses, their grudgingly-acknowledged merits written off as entirely technical.

The claim is not false as such, but the response to Edna and the reviews for this play mark the beginning of a desire to see plays which do not acknowledge their technical craft. From this springs an enduring myth of pure expression, untutored and spontaneous creativity, that appeared to find its form in the early works of Osborne, Wesker and Delaney. The truth is, surely, that the plays of the New Wave are also shaped by theatrical craft, albeit unacknowledged. The moral vision embodied by these later plays was one which valued authenticity over craft, while nonetheless using craft to make the case. Rattigan's error, if error it was, lay in his admission in 1953 that he consciously crafted his plays, that he worked with and against an audience's expectations; after 1956, it became conventional to pretend that the audience were of no importance in the construction and production of a play. And it is this latter view that was false, not Rattigan's.

Indeed in *Separate Tables*, the tension between Rattigan's care for the emotional complexity of character and his skill as a craftsman is itself pressed into service to deepen and enrich the events it describes. The play was written during a period in which Rattigan was struggling to negotiate very different impulses in his own life; the left-wing politics that he pursued in the 1930s were being challenged by a drift towards Liberalism; his homosexuality marked a kind of tangent from the rather exalted *haut bourgeois* circles of wealth and confidence in which he was moving; and as he moved into his forties, and towards middle age, he was no longer the rising young star of the British theatre. All of these tensions would be theatricalised in *Separate Tables*.

Frank Rattigan, Terry's father, had died three days after the opening of *The Deep Blue Sea*, in March 1952. That winter, Rattigan agreed to pay for his mother, Vera, to move closer to him, and put her up at a small residential hotel in Stanhope Gardens, South Kensington. Paul Bailey, in his introduction to Elizabeth Taylor's *Mrs Palfrey at the Claremont,* a novel which beautifully captures the final years of the residential hotel, refers to these curious institutions as 'chintz-bedecked battlegrounds'.[9] It was Rattigan's visits to his mother, in one of these sequestered, fading citadels of loneliness, that the idea for his new play began to form. The result was *Separate Tables,* comprising two one-act plays, originally titled *Table by the Window* and *Table by the Door*, the latter being retitled *Table Number Seven* during rehearsal. When published, the source and inspiration would be shyly acknowledged in Rattigan's dedication of the play to his mother.

Table by the Window deals with the relationship between John Malcolm, an ex-Labour MP, who spent time in prison for assaulting his wife, Anne Shankland, and who now lives a life of virtual anonymity, writing for a left-wing weekly, *New Outlook*, under the name 'Cato'. He is in a relationship with Miss Cooper, the manageress of the Beauregard Private Hotel, Bournemouth, where Anne turns up unexpectedly. Their successful reconciliation is disrupted when John discovers that her 'accidental' arrival was actually arranged, and he suspects her of trying to 'enslave' him again. But Miss Cooper, recognising the strength of feeling on both sides, gives way to Anne, and at the end of the play Anne and John have tentatively agreed to try again.

In the second piece, set in the same place but eighteen months later, the focus is now on Major David Pollock, a long-term, ex-public school resident who has struck up a curious friendship with Sibyl, the infantilised, terrorised, fragile daughter of the tyrannical Mrs Railton-Bell. Despite Pollock's best efforts to hide the report of it in the local newspaper, Mrs Railton Bell discovers that he has been arrested for molesting women in a cinema, and that his identity is largely confected: he never was a Major, never went to Wellington School. She calls a residents' meeting, and, despite many misgivings, they are railroaded into voting for Pollock's expulsion from the Hotel. Despite Miss Cooper's urging, Pollock prepares to leave. That evening the residents settle down to dinner and are surprised when Pollock also takes up his usual table. To Mrs Railton-Bell's horror, the residents, one by one, acknowledge Mr Pollock's presence, and tacitly accept him back into the hotel. When Sibyl herself, who had been utterly distraught and sickened by the news report, rebels against her mother, Mrs Railton-Bell leaves the dining room, and the diners continue with their meal.

It is instructive to see how Rattigan developed the two plays that make up *Separate Tables*. The earliest notes for the play take the form of several loose-leaf foolscap pages on which during 1953 he noted fragments of dialogue, gossip, and chatter.[10] From these small, isolated exchanges, a number of characters began to appear. On one page, Rattigan, with many crossings out and emendations, lists the following:

> Lady R + companion most money
> Eccentric. Dreams, sex, betting.
> Cheerful ~~Lady~~ down in the world, terribly poor, Lady D
> Boy girl. Undergraduates, married
> Retired schoolmaster - anxiously awaiting son who neglects
> Manageress Bright, cheerful ruthless and lonely "None of your sour-faced landladies"

In this list, it is already possible to see the genesis of Mrs Railton-Bell and Sibyl, as well as other residents of the Beauregard—Miss Meacham, Lady Matheson, Charles and Jean, Mr Fowler, and the manager, Miss Cooper. It is significant that the play emerged out of fragments of character and dialogue, because this is a key element of the play as a whole. *Separate Tables* introduces us to a network of characters and potential stories, such that it seems almost arbitrary that we follow one rather than another. The sense that there are other stories to tell accumulates a broader significance that enriches the individual stories that we are allowed to pursue. The double bill format, with its repetitions and parallels is an ideal form to explore this patterning of fragmentation and isolation; even so, and unlike his earlier double bill, *Harlequinade* and *The Browning Version*, the two plays are intimately connected, offering a fruitful tension between an individualistic focus on character and a more inclusive focus on narrative. Together, despite what Rattigan wrote in the *New*

Statesman, they form a sophisticated 'play of ideas' which addresses a much broader vision of society than its secluded setting might initially suggest.

Separate Tables begins as it ends, in the dining room of the Beauregard Private Hotel. This cosy bourgeois tableau is, however, carefully arranged to offer a landscape of solitude and isolation. Charles and Jean are sitting at the same table, but are both studiously reading. Miss Meacham is myopically inspecting the racing tips. Mr Fowler is alone at a table, 'quiet and impassive-looking' (p. 6). Mrs Railton-Bell's silver fox fur isolates her in her 'rather bare and quite unpretentious' surroundings (p. 5). The isolation of these characters, at their separate tables, is the background against which all subsequent events will unfold.

But while this one tone is established very quickly, the mood changes somewhat with the rumoured appearance of Anne. Characters relate brief sightings, comment on her dress and luggage, and offer their own prying speculations about her. This tells us something very clear about what we have seen: there are in fact connections between the characters, but they are on the level of gossip and surveillance. It gives the initial image of isolation a dangerous, fearful quality.

It is an extension of a technique Rattigan used in *The Deep Blue Sea*, to transform the conventional complacency of the West End 'room' into something darker, suggesting a refuge erected fearfully against the outside. Throughout *Separate Tables*, the devices used so often to move characters around the well-made play are put to different, more sophisticated ends. The telephone, so often pressed into service to give someone a convenient exit, is here poised on the threshold between the safety within and the danger without: its failure to ring crushes Mr Fowler; it reveals Anne's plan to John; and Mr Pollock, trying furtively to leave, finds himself trapped in the lounge of the Beauregard because Miss Meacham is on the phone in the corridor outside. Ironically, the hotel which was once his refuge has become a kind of prison.

This patterning of imprisonment and surveillance profoundly links *Separate Tables* to mid-century homosexual experience. In his book, *Discipline and Punish*, one of the major contemporary theorists of sexuality, Michel Foucault, argues that the form of the modern state was explicitly modelled on the Panopticon, a plan for a prison drawn up by the philosopher Jeremy Bentham. In the Panopticon, the cells are arranged in a circle around a central guard tower. The prisoners cannot see each other, but the guard can see all of the prisoners. Foucault argues that this structure induces in the prisoners a perpetual feeling of being watched that persists even when the guard is not in the tower. This observability is internalised by the prisoners, who thereby adopt the rules of the system. Foucault's later book, *The History of Sexuality: An Introduction*, discusses a nineteenth-century change in Western culture's handling of sex and sexuality. He argues that the standard images of Victorian sexual repression and silence are false; instead, during this era, people were encouraged to start seeing sexuality as a key part of their identities, which when confessed, revealed, brought out into the open, could help individuals understand themselves and others. But this mechanism for making sexuality visible, no less than the model of the Panopticon, was an operation of power, designed to control, not liberate.

This historical principle of trying to control illicit sexuality by making it visible had a particular force and relevance when Rattigan was writing *Separate Tables*. In the early 1950s, widespread scare stories had begun circulating in the press about an epidemic of homosexual activity. Partly precipitated by the surprisingly high figures of 'prevalence' published in the Kinsey Report on male sexuality in 1948, partly in response to pressure from the American government, still in the throes of the McCarthyite witchhunt against any form of political and sexual 'deviation', and also the flight to Russia of the homosexual spies, Burgess and MacLean, the press noted that the police were planning a crackdown on 'vice'. The 'problem' of homosexuality was that it was not immediately detectable; indeed, virtually all homosexuals were expert at 'passing' as straight. This flouting of the principles of the modern state seemed in need of address, and newspaper editorials and feature articles urged that 'it is necessary to turn the searchlight of publicity onto these abnormalities [...] Bringing the horrors of the situation out into the open is the first necessary step to getting control'.[11]

In this context, it becomes clear that much of the action of the play is metonymic of wider social conflicts. The campaign against 'vice' found its first major victim in October 1953, when the recently-knighted John Gielgud was arrested for importuning. About to make his first stage entrance after the arrest, he was reportedly paralysed with fear in the wings, until his co-star, Sybil Thorndike, came and pulled him out onto the stage, whereupon he was greeted with a standing ovation. The story of Major Pollock's arrest and of the support he finally wins from the residents was certainly inspired by the hounding and vindication of Rattigan's old friend. Naming Pollock's closest friend 'Sibyl' is almost certainly a discreet tribute to Thorndike's loyalty.[12]

Seen in historical context, the residents' gossip and tittle-tattle have therefore a harder edge. The Beauregard's status as a place of refuge is challenged by Mrs Railton-Bell's determination to bring the dominant moral evangelism of the outside world into the heart of the hotel. The kangaroo court that she peremptorily convenes to try David Pollock in his absence is explicitly compared by Charles to McCarthyism and Fascism. Mrs Railton-Bell says of Charles and Jean 'If they're in love, why don't they say so? I hate anything furtive' (p. 25), which is echoed by Charles in the debate about Pollock's crime, when he declares that he's 'always had an intense dislike of the more furtive forms of sexual expression' (p. 86). The obsession with bringing homosexuality out into the open was motivated by a desire to bring it under social control, though in the hands of certain MPs and the Wolfenden Committee (established in August 1954 to examine the law relating to sexual offences) it was often cloaked in the guise of liberalism. It is striking that this last declaration is spoken by the most liberal character in the play.[13]

But it is even more striking that Mrs Railton-Bell cloaks her own despotic prurience in the guise of solid civic virtue. Once she has forced the other residents to agree to Pollock's expulsion, she contemplates Charles's more sympathetic response to his predicament: 'what I say is—we're all of us entitled to our own opinions,' she announces open-mindedly, before adding darkly, 'however odd and dangerous and distasteful they may sometimes be'. And as she gleefully sets off to tell Miss Cooper of the residents' decision she adds gravely, 'I hope you all understand it's a duty I hardly relish' (p. 93). The preposterous hypocrisy of such statements is made clear by Rattigan's subtle, ironic interventions, especially in the final scene in the dining room, where Mrs Railton-Bell, apparently fatigued by the demands of good citizenship, declares: 'what a really nerve-racking day it's been hasn't it? I don't suppose any of us will ever forget it. Ever. I feel utterly shattered, myself. (*To* SIBYL.) Pass the sauce, dear' (p. 108), the incongruity of the final line wittily giving the lie to the rest. More cruelly, Mrs Railton-Bell takes great delight in telling Sibyl about Pollock's arrest, while contriving to ensure that it all appears to have been dragged unwillingly from her ('She insisted. She absolutely insisted' p. 83).

Nonetheless, some critics have claimed that, in not *directly* addressing homosexuality in this play and others, Rattigan 'funked it'.[14] His fear of letting his mother find out about his sexuality conspired to make him write a play which timidly avoided naming its real subject. However, to say this is to make precisely the same demands of *Separate Tables* that Mrs Railton-Bell makes of Mr Pollock. It is an approach to representation which will be satisfied with nothing but bringing homosexuality out into the open. The fact is that the play works in precisely the unsettling, subversive way that homosexuality operated in the 1950s; it hints at its subject matter, but makes it almost impossible to identify this subject clearly. In his biography of Rattigan, B. A. Young notes that the real subject of the play would have been clear to those members of the audience who wished to know.[15] Rattigan himself believed that most of them realised that the Major's actual crime was 'symbolical of another problem of which, at that time (just after several prominent cases), they were most sensitively conscious'.[16] Kenneth Tynan's review archly alludes to this double level of meaning when he has his 'Young Perfectionist' admit, 'I regretted that the major's crime was not something more cathartic than mere cinema flirtation. Yet I suppose the play is as good a handling of sexual abnormality as English playgoers will tolerate'.[17]

The Lord Chamberlain, in any case, would hardly have permitted a play which represented a homosexual on stage, let alone one which asked for tolerance and understanding.[18] Rattigan recognised this, explaining the mechanism of his play as a way round the censor's Panoptical scrutiny: 'I had in fact appealed over the head of the Lord Chamberlain to the sensibilities and particular awareness of an English audience. I was in fact saying to them, "Look, Ladies and Gentlemen, the Lord Chamberlain has forced me into an evasion, but you and I will foil him. Everybody in the play is going to behave as if there were no evasion at all and as if the more important and serious theme were still the issue"'.[19]

Which is precisely what the play does. Much of the dialogue seems far less relevant to Pollock's apparent crime than to a homosexual offence. When Jean bursts out in condemnation, Charles retorts, 'your vehemence is highly suspect. I must have you psychoanalysed' (p. 87), a clear reference to the then standard psychoanalytic belief that a person's extreme hostility to homo-sexuality could be traced to their own insufficiently repressed homosexual tendencies. The psychoanalytic model was for many people — including Rattigan — part of the 'common sense' understanding of homosexuality; one of its central beliefs was to explain homosexuality as a failure psychically to grow up, the dreadful result of a distant father and a dominant mother. This explains the bond between Sibyl and Pollock. With her dead father, dominating mother, and consequent infantilism, and his unusual sexual proclivities, homosexuality emerges associatively in the link between them. And Pollock's speech about having had to invent another personality is much more clearly pertinent to homosexual experience than it is to groping women in the dark.[20]

Understood in this way, the play can not only be interpreted as covertly 'about' homosexuality, but also as a play firmly resistant to the campaign to control it. In the face of crusades to open up homosexuality to public scrutiny, thereby removing its subversive ability to infiltrate and undermine the conventional pieties of sexual normality, the play's insistence on silence and calm is paradoxically radical. And the play does not isolate David Pollock; in fact, Rattigan carefully uses the other stories in the hotel to parallel and echo his predicament. Miss Cooper hides her relationship with John Malcolm, who himself has changed his name, and invented a further *nom de plume* for his political journalism. Charles and Jean studiously pretend to be friends and not lovers, even telling Charles's father a 'dirty lie' to make their relationship appear more respectable (p. 22); they also invent names for the other characters: Miss Meacham is 'Dream Girl', Mrs Railton-Bell 'Bournemouth Belle', Lady Matheson 'Minnie Mouse', John Malcolm 'Karl Marx' and Mr Fowler 'Mr Chips' (p. 21). This recognition that all of the characters have created personalities and roles for themselves echoes Pollock's adoption of pretended military rank and education. Even Mrs Railton-Bell's seizure of the moral high ground is ironically deflated by Charles with the words, 'Good God! What a performance' (p. 85). There is also a faint suggestion of homoeroticism in Mr Fowler's disappointed longing for his former pupils. After the bruising show-trial of Pollock, the residents decide to take their mind off things by going to watch Philip Harben's television cookery programme; as he leaves, Mr Fowler tries to illuminate the show's appeal: 'One suffers the tortures of Tantalus, and yet the pleasure is intense. Isn't that what is today called masochism?' (p. 94). It seems that perversity is not merely confined to Bournemouth's cinemas.

Rattigan's exquisite stagecraft turns the dynamics of the play slowly but surely against Mrs Railton-Bell. Her insistence on training the moral spotlight on 'Major' Pollock, is subtly under-mined, preparing us for her final defeat in the last scene. The first play begins with her failed attempts to strike up conversation. Her imperious efforts to determine the truth about pastry, betting and spiritualism are comically undermined by the unflappably eccentric Miss Meacham. Later, having foundered in her bid to correct John Malcolm on the rights and wrongs of socialism, the attempted magnificence of her theatrical exit is ruined, with Chekhovian bathos, by Lady Matheson's misplacement of her glasses (p. 29). She appears to fare better in the Pollock affair, yet Rattigan adroitly situates the audience at a distance from her; we are alerted to the presence of something in the local newspaper by Pollock's frantic attempt to remove all copies from the lounge, but he is foiled by Mrs Railton-Bell, whom we watch reading the newspaper: 'we do not see her face but the paper itself begins to shake slightly as she reads' (p. 77). The audience is informed of the report's contents when Lady Matheson reads it aloud; the effect is that when Mrs Railton-Bell makes her dramatic announcement to the residents, we already know the content and our focus is not on *what* is said, but *how* it is said. By separating our moment of revelation from that of the residents, Rattigan allows us critically to observe the mechanisms used to incite Pollock's removal from the hotel, to train the moral spotlight on the accuser rather than the accused.

But it is the final scene which most powerfully brings about Mrs Railton-Bell's downfall. The scene opens with the residents at dinner; Pollock appears to have left, his table is unlaid, and the 1950s strategy of controlling by making visible appears to have been effected. So, when he appears to take his usual table, it is a thrilling theatrical reversal.

Characteristically, the battle which commences is not verbally acknowledged by a single character, but is conducted with the weapons of the gaze; at a time when the ability of the straight world to control sexual deviancy through gazing fearlessly upon it was of widespread concern, this has a particular metaphorical force. When Pollock first appears, he cannot look anyone in the eye and he stares at the table cloth. Mrs Railton-Bell, on the other hand, 'is glaring furiously at him'. When Charles breaks the silence to address him, she turns 'fully round in her chair in an attempt to paralyse him into silence', and she is joined by Jean who is 'furiously glaring at her husband' (p. 109). When this appears to fail Mrs Railton-Bell decides to snub him by claiming to feel a imaginary draft and turning her chair so she has her back to him. This leaves her ill-prepared for Mr Fowler's move, as he interrupts his departure from the dining room to take a step back and acknowledge Mr Pollock. As a result, Mrs Railton-Bell is forced to 'twist her head sharply round in order to allow her eyes to confirm this shameful betrayal' (p. 110). Now Pollock is looking around the room; he catches the eye of Lady Matheson who involuntarily nods back to him, and then refuses to meet Mrs Railton-Bell's stare. In performance, the audience's eyes dart between Mrs Railton-Bell and her erstwhile victim, and it is Sibyl whose gaze resolves the contest. As Pollock appeared Sibyl had been staring at him; now she is staring at her mother. In this tightly-realized silent struggle of wills, Sibyl's simple response to her mother's attempt to take her out into the lounge—'No, Mummy' (p. 111)—clinches the dramatic shift in a quietly sensational *peripeteia*. The effect is to force this failed Medusa to essay a quietly dignified exit; but, as with John Malcolm, even this is unsuccessful as her exit is pre-empted by the sound of her daughter exchange pleasantries with her mother's intended victim.

The entire scene takes little more than five minutes of stage time, and the dialogue is all utterly banal, touching on nothing more dramatic than the weather, the racing, the cricket and the menu, yet the scene is powerfully emotional and joyously theatrical. The reversal of power is effected through the reversal of the gaze and completed by Mrs Railton-Bell's own expulsion from the stage space, and yet nothing appears to have been said. The rejection of the hostile gaze restores the kindlier relations subtly coded into the very name of the hotel Beauregard. And the play ends, as it began: 'a decorous silence, broken only by the renewed murmur of "the casuals", reigns once more, and the dining-room of the Beauregard Private Hotel no longer gives any sign of the battle that has just been fought and won between its four walls' (p. 113).

These subtextual dynamics have often encouraged critics to wonder if there were an earlier draft with Pollock's 'real' crime intact. Rumours of such first drafts have circulated around several of Rattigan's plays, notably *The Deep Blue Sea*, but have usually proved groundless. It is certainly the case that Rattigan originally conceived *Separate Tables* as one about a homosexual offence. He later claimed that so urgent was his desire to address the battles being waged around homosexuality in the 1950s that for a while he forgot about the censorship. 'I had already reached the point where the Major's offence was to be revealed before I realised that, if I were to get the play done in the West End at all, I would have to find a way round the Lord Chamberlain's present objection to any mention of this particular subject'.[21]

This would seem to have been the end of the story, were it not for the remarkable recent discovery in the Rattigan archive of an alternative version of *Separate Tables* with the homosexual subtext brought to the surface. It seems that in 1956, while preparing for the Broadway premiere, Rattigan had decided that, since no legal prohibition against homosexual representation existed on the New York stage, this was a good opportunity to restore Pollock's 'real' crime. Supported by various friends, including Alec Guinness, Laurence Olivier, Vivien Leigh, and Peter Glenville, he wrote to his American producer, Bob Whitehead, on 29 August 1956, with five new passages, that entirely alter the story of Pollock's arrest. Now he has been bound over at one in the morning after persistently importuning male persons on the Esplanade.

Whitehead was, however, uncomfortable about the changes. He claimed that they would place disproportionate emphasis on the new theme, and undoubtedly revive comment about Gielgud's arrest. More persuasively he noted that there had recently been several plays on the subject in New York and that it had 'almost become a cliché on the Broadway stage'.[22] This latter point was undoubtedly true, with *Tea and Sympathy* (1953) and *Cat on a Hot Tin Roof* (1955) being only the two most prominent Broadway plays addressing homosexuality. More crucially, Eric Portman, who was to reprise his roles as John Malcolm and David Pollock in the Broadway production, was himself gay, but was anxious, as many actors were, not to become associated with homosexuality in the public mind. As a result, Rattigan backed down. The alternative scenes remained unread and unperformed for almost forty years, until Geoffrey Wansell, researching for his 1995 biography unearthed them. This edition, for the first time, contains, alongside the familiar text, the full set of alternative scenes, which when substituted transform the story of Pollock's crime (see pp. 115-120).

A note of caution should be introduced, however; the 'gay version' is not the 'original version', as has been suggested elsewhere,[23] but rather a later revision, which postdates the earlier by some two and a half years. The first version, slyly coded and therefore operating over the head of the Lord Chamberlain, is much more in keeping with Rattigan's general style, and indeed fits more completely with the play's determination to promote the value of not making sexuality an object for public scrutiny and social control. More practically, while in the 1950s groping women in a cinema was clearly considered a lesser outrage than asking men for lights on the sea front, now audiences are surely inclined to look more sympathetically on the latter than the former. And so skilled is Rattigan's use of indirection, subtext and double-meaning, that the 'out' version of the play lacks the complexity of the semi-closeted one.

That said, there is considerable interest in the revised version of the play. The detail of the events as Rattigan recounts them, with the coded, conventional request for a light and the exchange of words leading to a 'certain suggestion' (p. 116), gives a glimpse of a whole area of homosexual experience with which Rattigan is clearly more familiar than he is with the business of molesting women in darkened rooms. In addition, certain aspects of the story take on a far clearer meaning. In the original, the woman who complains, Mrs Osborn, is mildly criticised by some of the residents; Charles finds 'her motives in complaining [...] extremely questionable' (p. 86). Apart from the general sense that she was vindictively making a nuisance of herself—a rather peculiar allegation—this comment is obscure. In the later version, however, the masculinized Mr Osborne has apparently admitted to having 'twice previously given evidence in Bournemouth in similar cases, but refused to admit that he had acted as "a stooge" for the police' (p. 116). The significance of this is even clearer in the original manuscript, in which Osborne denies that 'he had acted as "a stooge" for the police *against prosecution*'.[24] The suggestion here is that Mr Osborne is a homosexual who has been blackmailed by the police into entrapping others in exchange for immunity from prosecution. This and other deeply unethical forms of police activity were always denied at the time, yet were widely known to take place, often coming to light during the many high profile trials that marked the decade.[25]

It is ironic that *Separate Tables* should have gained the reputation of being the play that was written for Aunt Edna, since in both its versions it remains a complex challenge to the possible prejudices of this illustrious matriarch; ironic, too, because as well as being Rattigan's last play before the revolution marked by *Look Back in*

Anger, the first and often underrated part of *Separate Tables—Table by the Window*—bears an uncanny resemblance to Osborne's play. In Rattigan's manuscript notes, he describes it as the 'reverse of DBS'.[26] In *The Deep Blue Sea* Hester and Freddie are forced apart by the near-tragic consequences of their relationship, which Hester describes in terms of an evil affinity.[27] In *Table by the Window* we see a couple who have a similarly destructive effect on each other but who also cannot live apart. As Rattigan put in his notes, 'Better for evil affinity to continue to torture each other, than to be tortured alone'.[28] By the end of the first play, this mutually-destructive couple have uneasily decided to make a second attempt at being together, again preferring human contact, however precarious, to bleak isolation. In this, *Separate Tables* provides a link between the comic treatment of the same theme in Coward's *Private Lives* (1930),[29] and the brutally serious handling of it in *Look Back in Anger* (1956).[30]

With the plays written, the obvious choice of producer would normally have been the manager of H. M. Tennent Ltd., 'Binkie' Beaumont, the most powerful producer in the West End, who had presented many of Rattigan's premieres. But the two had fallen out over *The Sleeping Prince,* when Beaumont had dragged his feet over the casting of Olivier and Vivien Leigh, only relenting when Rattigan threatened to take the play elsewhere. Rattigan also felt Beaumont had been rather peremptory in curtailing the run when box office receipts dipped. Perhaps to remind Beaumont that he was not the only game in town, Rattigan sent *Separate Tables* to Stephen Mitchell, a rival producer who had presented *Playbill (The Browning Version* and *Harlequinade)* after Beaumont had rejected it. Rattigan had long promised, one day, to write a follow-up, and Mitchell set about reconvening the team that had made *Playbill* so successful. Peter Glenville, who had directed *Playbill* and *Adventure Story*, was brought in as director. Olivier and Vivien Leigh had wanted to play the leads, but Olivier was committed to filming *Richard III* and was thus unavailable, so Eric Portman, who had played Crocker-Harris and Arthur Gosport in *Playbill,* was brought back to play Malcolm and the 'Major'. Mary Ellis, who had proved somewhat difficult in 1948, was passed over in favour of Kay Walsh. Yet as rehearsals began, Walsh seemed increasingly unsuited to the roles of Anne and Sybil, and, rather than risk his new play, Rattigan asked that Glenville replace her with Margaret Leighton, an actress that Rattigan had long admired (and whom he had failed to persuade Frith Banbury to cast as Hester Collyer in *The Deep Blue Sea*). Another welcome feature of the production was the return to the stage of Phyllis Neilson-Terry (as Mrs Railton-Bell) and Jane Eccles (as Lady Matheson), after nine and twenty years, respectively.

A new Terence Rattigan play was always a major theatrical event
in the 1950s, and the opening at the St James's Theatre, on 22
September 1954, following a month-long pre-London tour, was
accompanied by a rush of publicity, and some excellent reviews.
Harold Hobson thought *Table Number Seven* 'one of Mr
Rattigan's masterpieces, in which he shows in a superlative
degree his pathos, his humour, and his astounding mastery over
that English language whose riches he despises,' the last comment
being a somewhat mealy-mouthed tribute to Rattigan's ability to
produce enormous emotional resonance from the trivia of
ordinary conversation. All critics joined Gerard Fay in admiring
the 'boastful ease' with which Eric Portman and Margaret
Leighton effected their transitions from one play to the other.
Leighton's transformation from the glamorous model of the first
half to the mousey, downtrodden creature of the second caused
particular comment; at least two tabloids ran features in which
Leighton offered make-up tips on how to avoid looking like the
dowdy Sibyl.[31] Looking at contemporary responses reminds us
that in 1954, Britain was still in the final throes of rationing, as
one newspaper drools that real food, including authentic hot
buttered toast, is being used in the production. The production ran
for 726 performances, and numbered among its first audience the
Queen Mother and Princess Margaret, which we have to
understand was then a rather impressive and prestigious mark of
theatrical success.

The production, with a few minor alterations to the cast (though
none, of course, to the script), opened at the Music Box Theatre,
New York, on 25 October 1956. The production managed to
overcome Broadway's usual resistance to Rattigan's work; Brooks
Atkinson in the *New York Times* called it 'the most penetrating
enquiry into the human spirit that Mr Rattigan has yet written, and
it considerably alters his reputation as a theatre writer'. Richard
Watts, in the *New York Post*, found 'beneath the sparkling surface
of showmanship [...] dramatic writing of notable insight, sympathy,
emotional truth and keenly observing intelligence'. *Variety*'s
prediction that the play would be a 'smash' was proved correct: the
production ran for almost a year on Broadway, followed by a six-
month national tour. Revivals soon appeared, including a
production at the Paper Mill Playhouse in Millburn, New Jersey,
starring Basil Rathbone and Geraldine Page.[32]

Rattigan sold the film rights for over a third of a million dollars to
independent producers Harold Hecht and Burt Lancaster. The
result is widely regarded as the finest screen adaptation of a
Rattigan play. Directed by Delbert Mann, and starring Burt
Lancaster as an Americanized John Malcolm, Deborah Kerr as
Sibyl, David Niven as Mr Pollock, Rita Hayworth as Ann
Shankland, Wendy Hiller as Miss Cooper and Gladys Cooper as

Mrs Railton-Bell, the film was nominated for seven Oscars: best picture, actor (Niven), actress (Kerr), supporting actress (Hiller), adapted screenplay, cinematography, and musical score, with Niven and Hiller winning in their categories. In America, *Separate Tables* remains Rattigan's best-known and most-admired play.[33]

The subsequent British performance history of *Separate Tables* follows the usual pattern of Rattigan's work. A number of touring and repertory productions immediately followed the end of the West End run. There were productions in Wimbledon, Richmond and Brighton in 1956, and in Bromley, Aberdeen, Derby and Dundee in 1957 amongst others. But major revivals dried up by the mid-sixties and between 1966 and 1973, no productions are recorded.

The first West End revival came in the seventies, during a short-lived wave of revivals of Rattigan plays and reputation. A two-and-a-half-month tour of the play eventually worked its way into London at the Apollo Theatre early in 1977, directed by Michael Blakemore, who unnecessarily retitled the plays *Table Number One* and *Table Number Two*. The production starred John Mills and Jill Bennett—then, ironically, married to John Osborne—in the leads and Margaret Courtney and Zena Walker as Mrs Railton-Bell and Miss Cooper. Critics generally seemed to find Jill Bennett unconvincing as Sibyl, B. A. Young in the *Financial Times* explaining 'I do not think she has it in her to be inadequate'. The meticulous construction of the second half was now an obstacle to many critics; the *Daily Telegraph* found the writing 'obtrusively neat' and 'cunningly contrived' though many agreed with the *Observer*'s detection of 'good Strindbergian stuff' in the first-half battle between John and Anne. The feeling remained that this was a period piece. In *Punch*'s theatre listings, the play was summarily dismissed with the line 'two-star hotel in Hampshire, residents exquisitely embalmed'.[34]

The next major revival came in 1993, hard on the heels of the Almeida's magnificent, revelatory *Deep Blue Sea*. Peter Hall, directing the piece at the Albery Theatre, attempted to find in it a 'state of the nation' play about Britain at the twilight of its Empire; a faded Union Jack hung on the wall, and the play was punctuated with the playing of 'Jerusalem'. The echoes and patterns of Pollock's predicament were pointed up by Miriam Karlin, who played Miss Meacham, in Nicholas de Jongh's words, as a 'brisk, no-nonsense lesbian'. Critics were divided; Robert Hewison found Hall's production reluctant to bring the emotional drama sufficiently near the surface, while Charles Spencer in the *Daily Telegraph* wrote: 'I suspect 1993 will be remembered as the year Terence Rattigan finally came in from the cold', and, in a satisfying revision of the first critics' objections, described the portrait of Mrs Railton-Bell as 'Rattigan's revenge on Aunt Edna'.

The craftsmanship was less of a deterrent than it had been in 1977, and Billington in the *Guardian* was moved to remark that 'when the hotel bigot [...] is routed, one can scarce forbear to cheer'. The production also coincided with revivals of Coward's *Present Laughter* and Osborne's *Inadmissible Evidence*, leading Malcolm Rutherford in the *Financial Times* to argue that 'if you look at the playwrights as a group, it is their continuity that stands out'.[35]

The King's Head Theatre, where Rattigan's reassessment as a serious dramatist had started in 1976 with a pared-down revival of *The Browning Version*, offered another landmark production in 1998. This paired *Harlequinade* with *Table Number Seven*, but for the first time was able to present the revised, 'gay version' of the latter. Colin Ellwood's production softened the sharp transition between the two plays with a brief dumbshow miming the games of coded seduction on the sea-front that illustrated Pollock's own nocturnal stroll. Barbara Jefford's splendidly beady-eyed Mrs Railton-Bell suitably dominated Lucy Whybrow's stammeringly intense Sibyl, and Barry Wallman's Major Pollock suggested a man drained of courage by a life of subterfuge and performance. The critics were generally united in their admiration of what was, after all, a posthumous Rattigan premiere, Nicholas de Jongh noting 'how luminously Rattigan evokes the sexually intolerant and phobic attitudes of Fifties middle England' and Kate Bassett welcoming the newfound sense of 'personal passion behind the heated ethical debate'.[36]

Separate Tables is perhaps the play of Rattigan's that was most damaged by the shrapnel flung out during the explosive realignment of British theatrical tastes in the mid-fifties. Long dismissed as a cosy warhorse, or melodramatic potboiler, the play hides beneath its immaculate and beautifully-wrought surface a dark and uncomfortable portrait of sexual oppression. Its delight in subtext, in tacit revolt, in silence is not a plea for an easy life, or an apology for quietism or emotional apathy; in its carefully crafted tales of rejection and reconciliation, it offers a vision of a tolerant, caring community, in which the vicious bonds of gossip and surveillance are replaced by those of understanding and respect. Its intervention into debates about the social control of sexuality are made with disarming delicacy yet great theatrical force, offering a quietly radical call for compassion and resistance to the forces of sexual persecution.

Notes

1. Terence Rattigan. 'Concerning the Play of Ideas.' *New Statesman and Nation*. (4 March 1950). pp. 242.

2. George Bernard Shaw. 'The Play of Ideas.' *New Statesman and Nation*. (6 May 1950), p. 510.

3. Terence Rattigan. 'The Play of Ideas.' *New Statesman and Nation*. (13 May 1950), p. 546.

4. Terence Rattigan. Introduction. *Collected Plays: Volume Two*. London: Hamish Hamilton, 1953, p. viii.

5. Dan Rebellato. *1956 and All That: The Making of Modern British Drama*. London: Routledge, 1999, pp. 104-113.

6. cf. Joe Orton. *The Orton Diaries*. Edited by John Lahr. London: Methuen, 1986, pp. 271- 289.

7. All reviews, unless otherwise stated, from the Production File for *Separate Tables*. St. James's Theatre. 22 September 1954, in the Theatre Museum, London.

8. Kenneth Tynan. *Tynan on Theatre*. Penguin, 1964, p. 30.

9. Paul Bailey. Introduction. *Mrs Palfrey at the Claremont*, by Elizabeth Taylor. London: Virago, 1982 [originally published, 1971], p. x.

10. The Rattigan Archive at the British Library, which is not yet fully catalogued, contains a large assortment of these handwritten notes for *Separate Tables* in an envelope marked 'Table by the Window / Table by the Door / + / notes etc'. I must record my gratitude to Sally Brown at the British Library for her patient help in retrieving material from the archive.

11. Douglas Warth. 'Evil Men—Pt 2' *Sunday Pictorial*, (25 May 1952), p. 15.

12. There are several other such personal references in the play. The name of the street on which the Beauregard Hotel stands is Morgan Crescent, and the complainant in the cinema (and in the alternative version on the Esplanade) is called Osborne. Kenneth Morgan and Peter Osborne were former lovers of Rattigan's. The relationship between John and Anne was probably part-inspired by Rattigan's new partner, and in the name Shankland one can hear a distinct echo of his name: Michael Franklin. (He reappears, in the gay version of the second play, in the name of Pollock's arresting officer.) The hotel to which David Pollock briefly considers going is in West Kensington, which one may fancifully speculate could have made him a fellow resident of Rattigan's mother. The character of the 'Major' was perhaps also inspired by Rattigan's father, also a Major, with an actively adulterous (though strictly heterosexual) sex life. Anne Shankland was also based on Rattigan's friend, the model Jean Dawnay, who had a similarly violent domestic life; indeed, so close was the resemblance that Dawnay had to ask Rattigan to redraw the portrait to make it less obvious.

13. The portrayal of Charles and Jean—the 'transients'—complicates and deepens both stories. Jean's 'modern' insistence on wanting a career before marriage or children echoes Anne in the first act, though the beginning of the second play shows that these principles have not been adhered to. In the first they appear as projections of the young John and Anne. By the second, their secret conventionality contrasts with Pollock's more genuine sexual outsiderliness.

14. Nicholas de Jongh. *Not in Front of the Audience: Homosexuality on Stage*. London: Routledge, 1992, p. 58.

15. B. A. Young. *The Rattigan Version: Sir Terence Rattigan and the Theatre of Character*. London: Hamish Hamilton, 1986, p. 91.

16. Quoted in Geoffrey Wansell. *Terence Rattigan: A Biography*. London: Fourth Estate, 1995, p. 258

17. Tynan, *op. cit.,* p. 30.

18. Of course, his play could have been produced in a club theatre, but there it would have joined a long list of plays earnestly discussing the 'problem' of homosexuality, including Andrew Rosenthal's *Third Person*, Julien Green's *South*, Lillian Hellman's *The Children's Hour*, Roger Gellert's *Quaint Honour*, Ronald Duncan's *The Catalyst*, Philip King's *Serious Charge*, and Philip King and Robin Maugham's *The Lonesome Road*. These 'thesis' plays had their strengths, but *Separate Tables* would have been lost amongst them.

19. Quoted in Wansell, *op. cit.,* pp. 273-274. For the record, the Lord Chamberlain certainly did not suspect that Pollock's crime could be anything other than is expressly stated. The reader, Geoffrey Dearmer, wrote of *Table By the Door* (as the second half was still titled when submitted for licence), 'This is much the better of the two, I think being in no way far-fetched in plot. It is a little masterpiece' Reader's Report, 24 July 1954, *Separate Tables*. Lord Chamberlain's Correspondence: 1954/6930. [British Library].

20. In a letter to his American producer in 1956, Rattigan listed a whole raft of lines which are obviously responses to a homosexual, not a heterosexual, offence. cf. Wansell, *op. cit.*, p. 274.

21. Letter from Rattigan to Bob Whitehead, August 1956, quoted in *ibid.,* p. 253.

22. Quoted in *ibid.*, p. 276.

23. This claim was made in a newspaper article discussing the premiere of the gay version of *Separate Tables*, Dan Glaister, 'Rattigan and the curious case of the gay major,' *Guardian,* (26 February 1998), p. 3, and also in the revised reissue of Rattigan *Plays: One*. London: Methuen, 1999, p. xvi.

24. My emphasis. The variants in both manuscript and typescript forms (with some manuscript notes) are contained in a single file in the Rattigan archive in the British Library. In the manuscript from which Mary Herring (Rattigan's secretary) worked to prepare the typescript, the last two words have been struck out.

25. An editorial, 'The Police and the Montagu Case' in the *New Statesman and Nation* xlvii, 1205 (10 April 1954), pp. 456-457, discussed one very high-profile trial and claimed that Lord Montagu was being persecuted by the police; at his original trial, the jury were unable to reach a verdict, no doubt partly because an important piece of evidence, a visa stamp in Montagu's passport, was clearly a forgery, almost certainly perpetrated by the police in whose possession the document had lain for three months. The editorial also noted that Major Pitt-Rivers, another defendant, had his flat searched without a warrant. The airmen, with whom the defendants were supposed to have committed homosexual offences, 'were known to have been similarly involved with twenty-four other men, none of whom was charged' (p. 456). But because they turned (to use the unfortunate phrase) 'Queen's Evidence' they had been granted immunity from prosecution. See also H. Montgomery Hyde. *The Other Love: An Historical and Contemporary Survey of Homosexuality in Britain*. London: Heinemann, 1970, pp. 215-225.

26. See note 10..

27. Terence Rattigan. *The Deep Blue Sea*. London: Nick Hern, 1999, p. 61.

28. See note 10.

29. There is an obvious affinity between Amanda, in Coward's *Private Lives*, describing her relationship with Elyot 'like two violent acids bubbling away in a nasty little matrimonial bottle' (*Collected Plays: Two*. London:

Methuen, 1999, p. 16) and John's suggestion that he and Anne are 'like two chemicals that are harmless by themselves, but when brought together in a test-tube can make an explosive as deadly as dynamite' (p. 60).

30. According to his autobiography, Osborne told George Devine that he had 'no high opinion of *Separate Tables*', (*Almost a Gentleman: An Autobiography, Vol 2: 1955-1966*. London: Faber and Faber, 1991, p. 9) yet John Malcolm, with his impetuous honesty, his North Country accent, and his hatred of agony aunt columns and his mother-in-law, bears a profound resemblance to Jimmy Porter, the anti-hero of *Look Back in Anger*. John's sympathy for the impoverished aristocrat, Lady Matheson, has affinities with Jimmy's curious empathy for the faded colonial administrator, Colonel Redfern, and Jimmy and Alison, like John and Anne, break up and reunite at the end of their plays, despite the men's claims that their partners have almost hypnotic powers of control, and that they use it to break down and consume the men they meet. Rattigan's notorious suggestion, on the steps of the Royal Court, that *Look Back in Anger* was burdened by a desire to avoid resembling Rattigan's work is perhaps more legitimate than has generally been thought.

31. 'Yes!—A Woman's A Two-Face,' *Daily Express*. (27 September 1954); Iris Ashley, 'Hello Folks!' *Daily Mail*. (15 November 1954). Articles to be found in the Production File for *Separate Tables*. St James's Theatre. 22 September 1954, in the Theatre Museum, London.

32. Reviews quoted from Wansell, *op. cit.,* pp. 278, 280. Many thanks to David Travis and Ginny Bull for information about American productions.

33. American critic, Susan Rusinko, calls it 'Rattigan's major drama'. *Terence Rattigan*. English Authors, 366. Boston: Twayne, 1983, p. 93.

34. Reviews quoted from the Production File for *Separate Tables*. Apollo Theatre. 17 January 1977, in the Theatre Museum, London.

35. Reviews quoted from *Theatre Record*, xiii, 14 (24 July 1993), pp. 765-770.

36. Reviews quoted from *Theatre Record,* xviii 7 (27 April 1998), pp. 415-417.

List of Rattigan's Produced Plays

Title	British Première	New York Première
First Episode (with Philip Heimann)	'Q' Theatre, Surrey, 11 Sept 1933, trans. Comedy Th, 26 January 1934	Ritz Theatre 17 September 1934
French Without Tears	Criterion Th, 6 Nov 1936	Henry Miller Th, 28 Sept 1937
After the Dance	St James's Th, 21 June 1939	
Follow My Leader (with Anthony Maurice, alias Tony Goldschmidt)	Apollo Th, 16 Jan 1940	
Grey Farm (with Hector Bolitho)		Hudson Th, 3 May 1940
Flare Path	Apollo Th, 13 Aug 1942	Henry Miller Th, 23 Dec 1942
While the Sun Shines	Globe Th, 24 Dec 1943	Lyceum Th, 19 Sept 1944
Love in Idleness	Lyric Th, 20 Dec 1944	Empire Th (as *O Mistress Mine*), 23 Jan 1946
The Winslow Boy	Lyric Th, 23 May 1946	Empire Th, 29 October 1947
Playbill (The Browning Version, Harlequinade)	Phoenix Th, 8 Sept 1948	Coronet Th, 12 October 1949
Adventure Story	St James's Th, 17 March 1949	
A Tale of Two Cities (adapt from Dickens, with John Gielgud)	St Brendan's College Dramatic Scy, Clifton, 23 Jan 1950	
Who is Sylvia?	Criterion Th, 24 Oct 1950	
Final Test (tv)	BBC TV 29 July 1951	

The Deep Blue Sea	Duchess Th, 6 March 1952	Morosco Th, 5 Nov 1952
The Sleeping Prince	Phoenix Th, 5 November 1953	Coronet Th, 1 November 1956
Separate Tables (*Table by the Window, Table Number Seven*)	St James's Th, 22 Sept 1954	Music Box Th, 25 Oct 1956
Variation on a Theme	Globe Th, 8 May 1958	
Ross	Theatre Royal, Hay-market, 12 May 1960	Eugene O'Neill Th, 26 Dec 1961
Joie de Vivre (with Robert Stolz, Paul Dehn)	Queen's Th, 14 July 1960	
Heart to Heart (tv)	BBC TV, 6 Dec 1962	
Man and Boy	Queen's Th, 4 Sept 1963	Brooks Atkinson Th, 12 Nov 1963
Ninety Years On (tv)	BBC TV, 29 Nov 1964	
Nelson – a Portrait in Miniature (tv)	Associated Television, 21 March 1966	
All on Her Own (tv) [adapted for stage as *Duologue*]	BBC 2, 25 Sept 1968 King's Head, Feb 1976	
A Bequest to the Nation	Theatre Royal, Hay-market, 23 Sept 1970	
High Summer (tv)	Thames TV, 12 Sept 1972	
In Praise of Love (*After Lydia, Before Dawn*)	Duchess Th, 27 Sept 1973	Morosco Th, 10 Dec 1974
Cause Célèbre (radio)	BBC Radio 4 27 Oct 1975	
Cause Célèbre (stage)	Her Majesty's Th, 4 July 1977	

SEPARATE TABLES

TO MY MOTHER

Editor's Note

Separate Tables exists in two different versions,
as explained in the Introduction.

The text that follows is the 'standard' version,
which first appeared in Rattigan's *Collected Plays*
and has formed the basis of all subsequent editions.
Where a passage exists in a variant version,
a line appears in the margin alongside that passage.
The variant version is printed in an appendix
at the end of the play.

Separate Tables was first produced at the St. James's Theatre, London, on 22 September 1954, with the following cast:

TABLE BY THE WINDOW

MABEL	Marion Fawcett
LADY MATHESON	Jane Eccles
MRS. RAILTON-BELL	Phyllis Neilson-Terry
MISS MEACHAM	May Hallatt
DOREEN	Priscilla Morgan
MR. FOWLER	Aubrey Mather
MRS. SHANKLAND	Margaret Leighton
MISS COOPER	Beryl Measor
MR. MALCOLM	Eric Portman
CHARLES STRATTON	Basil Henson
JEAN TANNER	Patricia Raine

TABLE NUMBER SEVEN

JEAN STRATTON	Patricia Raine
CHARLES STRATTON	Basil Henson
MAJOR POLLOCK	Eric Portman
MR. FOWLER	Aubrey Mather
MISS COOPER	Beryl Measor
MRS. RAILTON-BELL	Phyllis Neilson-Terry
MISS RAILTON-BELL	Margaret Leighton
LADY MATHESON	Jane Eccles
MISS MEACHAM	May Hallatt
MABEL	Marion Fawcett
DOREEN	Priscilla Morgan

The plays directed by Peter Glenville
Decor by Michael Weight

The action of both plays takes place in the Lounge and Dining-Room of the Beauregard Private Hotel, near Bournemouth.

TABLE BY THE WINDOW

Characters

in order of speaking

MABEL
LADY MATHESON
MRS. RAILTON-BELL
MISS MEACHAM
DOREEN
MR. FOWLER
MRS. SHANKLAND
MISS COOPER
MR. MALCOLM
CHARLES STRATTON
JEAN TANNER

Time: Winter.

Scene One: Dining-Room. Dinner.
Scene Two: Lounge. After Dinner.
Scene Three: Dining-Room. Breakfast.

5

Scene One

*Scene: the dining-room of the Beauregard Private Hotel, near
Bournemouth. It is small, rather bare and quite unpretentious. A
door at back leads into the lounge, a swing door upstage right
into the kitchen, and another downstage right into the hall and
the rest of the hotel. Windows, left, are curtained at the moment,
for it is a winter evening, about seven o'clock, and the guests
are at dinner.*

Each sits at a small separate table, except for a young couple,
CHARLES STRATTON *and* JEAN TANNER, *who, as mere
transients, occupy a table together in a corner of the room, not
garnished, as are the other tables, with the bottles of medicine
and favourite pickles and other idiosyncratic personal
accessories of the permanent residents. Surprisingly, for they
are an attractive-looking pair,* CHARLES *and* JEAN *are paying
no attention to each other at all, and each is avidly reading a
book propped up on the flower vase between them.*

*Prominently placed, and indeed a rather prominent-looking
person altogether, is* MRS. RAILTON-BELL. *All the ladies
(except* JEAN *who wears slacks) always change 'into
something' for dinner, but* MRS. RAILTON-BELL *always
changes into something much grander than the others. All the
ladies (except* JEAN) *wear fur stoles, but* MRS. RAILTON-
BELL *wears silver foxes. All the ladies (except* JEAN) *wear
some small items of jewellery, but* MRS. RAILTON-BELL's *are
far less small than the others.*

MISS MEACHAM *sits near her, reading (very close to her
unspectacled eyes) a copy of 'Racing Up To Date'. Although
much the same age as* MRS. RAILTON-BELL *(about sixty-five)
she is dressed in a far more sprightly fashion, but has not
succeeded in looking any younger.*

LADY MATHESON, *a Civil Servant's widow, living on an annuity and therefore the poorest of all the residents, sits close by, a grey-faced, mousy, impeccably dressed woman, rather younger than the other two.* MR. FOWLER, *ex-public-school master, quiet and impassive-looking, sits further away.*

The table by the window is unoccupied – as is another towards the centre of the room and close to MRS. RAILTON-BELL.

Two waitresses, one middle-aged (MABEL) *the other young* (DOREEN), *serve the various tables.* MABEL *is taciturn, gloomy and dependable.* DOREEN *is flighty, talkative and undependable. At the moment only* MABEL *is visible. She is serving* LADY MATHESON.

MABEL. Were you medaillon or goulash?

LADY MATHESON (*correctly accenting*). Medaillon.

MABEL. Sorry. I thought you were goulash.

She stumps with the unwanted goulash to the kitchen door.

LADY MATHESON. It was probably my fault.

MABEL (*gloomily*). I dare say.

She passes on to MISS MEACHAM.

Now, you *were* goulash, weren't you, Miss Meacham?

MISS MEACHAM (*deep in her book*). What? Oh yes, Mabel. Thank you.

MABEL (*serving her*). And what to follow – the mousse angelic, or the turnover?

MISS MEACHAM. Which do you think?

MABEL. Turnover.

MISS MEACHAM. Turnover, then.

MABEL *drifts away.*

MRS. RAILTON-BELL. I think cook's acquiring a little lighter touch with her pastry, don't you think?

MISS MEACHAM. Not judging by the tarts we had at tea yesterday. Cannon-balls.

MRS. RAILTON-BELL. Did you think so? I quite liked them. I much preferred them to those pink cakes on Tuesday.

MISS MEACHAM. I didn't mind the pink cakes. The tarts gave me the collywobbles. I had the most terrible dreams.

MRS. RAILTON-BELL (*with a faint smile*). I thought you were always having dreams.

MISS MEACHAM. Oh, these weren't my proper dreams. Not the ones I make myself dream. These were just horrible, pointless nightmares. Cosh boys and things. (*After a slight pause.*) I talked to Louis XV on Thursday night.

MRS. RAILTON-BELL (*plainly humouring her*). Did you indeed, dear?

MISS MEACHAM. The goulash's rather good. I think you made a mistake.

She goes back to her book. There is a silence for a few moments while MISS MEACHAM *peruses her 'Racing Up To Date' with myopic concentration.*

MRS. RAILTON-BELL. Think you've found a winner for tomorrow, Miss Meacham?

MISS MEACHAM. Well, according to this form book, Marston Lad is worth a bob or two each way.

MRS. RAILTON-BELL. I never bet nowadays. (*After a meditative pause.*) When my husband was alive he used sometimes to put as much as five pounds on a horse for me.

MISS MEACHAM (*looking up*). I used to bet in ponies when my father was alive, and I had an allowance.

She goes back to her 'Racing Up To Date'.

MRS. RAILTON-BELL (*suddenly irritable*). Why don't you get spectacles?

MISS MEACHAM *lowers her book.*

MISS MEACHAM. Because I don't need them.

She goes back to her book again. DOREEN, *the other waitress, has come in and is now hovering over* MR. FOWLER.

DOREEN. Sorry, Mr. Fowler, the goulash's off.

MR. FOWLER *looks up abstractedly.*

MR. FOWLER. What? Oh. What about the cold pie?

DOREEN. I shouldn't have that, if I were you. I saw what went into it. If I were you I'd have the tongue –

MR. FOWLER. All right. Whatever you say.

DOREEN *disappears into the kitchen.*

MRS. RAILTON-BELL (*to* LADY MATHESON, *meaningly*). She won't last.

LADY MATHESON. I'm afraid not.

MRS. RAILTON-BELL. Still, it's disgraceful that the goulash's off, and two people not even in yet.

LADY MATHESON. I know.

MRS. RAILTON-BELL. Of course Mr. Malcolm's never on time, (*She indicates the table by the window.*) and really deserves it. (*In another confidential whisper.*) Anyway, after those long sessions at the Feathers I often wonder if he ever really knows what he's eating. But the new lady (*She indicates the other unoccupied table.*) – I mean, my dear, what will she think?

LADY MATHESON. I saw her arrive.

MRS. RAILTON-BELL. Did you?

LADY MATHESON. Did you?

MRS. RAILTON-BELL (*slightly annoyed*). I was in the lounge, but I didn't – excuse me – think it quite the thing to peer out of the window at her –

LADY MATHESON (*firmly*). I happened to be in the hall.

MISS MEACHAM. I met her on the stairs.

MRS. RAILTON-BELL. Really, dear?

MISS MEACHAM (*still absorbed in her book*). She's called Mrs. Shankland. She comes from London, she arrived by train, she has four suitcases and a hatbox and she's staying two weeks.

MRS. RAILTON-BELL (*unwillingly impressed*). Four suitcases?

MISS MEACHAM. And a hatbox.

LADY MATHESON. She was awfully smartly dressed. Nothing flashy – very good taste – but – well – Mayfair, if you know what I mean.

MRS. RAILTON-BELL. Really? (*Changing the subject from this unwelcome topic.*) It was quite nice out this afternoon, didn't you think, dear – I mean, for December?

LADY MATHESON. I didn't go out, I'm afraid. There was a Sibelius concert on the Home –

MRS. RAILTON-BELL. You and your music. Did you go out, Mr. Fowler?

MR. FOWLER. What? No, I didn't. I was waiting for a telephone call.

MRS. RAILTON-BELL. I was the only brave one then? Fancy.

She breaks off abruptly as the door from the hall opens and MRS. SHANKLAND (ANNE), *the new arrival, comes in. She is about forty, and, as she stands just inside the room looking around rather timidly, she seems entirely out of place in such an environment. Not that her clothes are unsuitable, although they are smart, nor that her coiffure is too stylish, although it is stylish, but that she has brought on with her an air of Belgravia and the smarter London restaurants. She stands now as if waiting for a head waiter to guide her to her table. None of the other guests glance at her.* MABEL, *who is serving* MISS MEACHAM *with her turnover, turns and sees her.*

MABEL. You're the new one, aren't you?

ANNE. Yes.

MABEL. You're here.

She points to the table in the centre.

ANNE. Oh. Thank you.

She goes to the table and sits down. Dead silence still reigns. MABEL *hands her a menu and, while she is studying it, eyes begin to cast quick, furtive glances in her direction.*

MABEL. The brown windsor or the petite marmite?

ANNE. I don't think I'll have any soup, thank you. I'll try the goulash.

MABEL. That's right. We've got a portion left.

MR. FOWLER *glares furiously at* MABEL *as she goes past him to the kitchen, but decides not to make a scene. Eyes are lowered again as* ANNE *looks curiously round the room. The silence continues until it is at length broken by* MRS RAILTON-BELL, *speaking now in a rather louder and more self-consciously well-bred voice than before.*

MRS. RAILTON-BELL (*to* LADY MATHESON). I was saying about the weather in December –

LADY MATHESON. Oh yes?

MRS. RAILTON-BELL. It can be so treacherous, especially here, on the south coast. This afternoon, for instance, even though the sun was quite bright, I put on a fur coat – my warmest one too – the Persian Lamb.

LADY MATHESON. Very sensible of you.

The two young people rise abruptly and make for the lounge door, each carrying their book. They have still, as far as we can see, not addressed a word to each other. MRS. RAILTON-BELL *eyes them with disdain.*

MRS. RAILTON-BELL. Trousers at dinner!

LADY MATHESON. I know.

MRS RAILTON-BELL. And *he* never changes either. I wonder Miss Cooper doesn't say something. You'd think they'd teach them better manners at Oxford.

LADY MATHESON. Yes, you would. (*After a slight pause.*) My husband was at Oxford.

MRS. RAILTON-BELL (*gently*). Yes, dear. You've told me so before. Mine only went to Birmingham because of the wonderful engineering course they have there. He hated it, of course.

MISS COOPER *has come in and is crossing the room towards* ANNE. *She is youngish, with a rather masculine appearance and a quiet manner.*

MISS COOPER. Good evening, Mrs. Railton-Bell.

MRS. RAILTON-BELL. Good evening, Miss Cooper.

MISS COOPER. Good evening, Lady Matheson.

LADY MATHESON. Good evening.

MISS MEACHAM *does not look up.* MISS COOPER *continues her journey towards* ANNE's *table.*

MISS COOPER. Is everything all right, Mrs. Shankland?

ANNE. Yes, thank you.

MISS COOPER. I'm so sorry I wasn't here to show you your table. I had a telephone call from London. Are you being looked after all right?

ANNE. Yes, thank you.

MABEL *has brought her dish and now places it before her.*

MISS COOPER (*sharply*). No soup?

ANNE. No. I don't care for it. It's bad for the figure.

MISS COOPER. I shouldn't have thought you'd have to worry about that, Mrs. Shankland.

ANNE. Oh, I do. I work at modelling, you know.

MISS COOPER. And now you're down here for a little rest?

ANNE. Yes. That's right.

MISS COOPER. I hope you find your room quite comfortable.

ANNE. I'm sure I shall.

MISS COOPER. If there's anything you want please don't hesitate to ask me.

ANNE. I won't.

MISS COOPER *flashes her a cordial smile, extinguished instantly as she turns away. She glances at the empty table by the window, and summons* MABEL *with a gesture.*

MISS COOPER. Mabel, go to Mr. Malcolm's room and tell him –

MABEL. I've been. He's not there.

MISS COOPER. Oh. Have they kept something hot for him?

MABEL. Yes, but cook says if he's not in in five minutes he'll have to have cold.

MISS COOPER. Oh, well, I don't expect he'll be more than that.

MABEL *looks unconvinced.* MISS COOPER *goes towards the hall door.* MR. FOWLER, *rising from his table, intercepts her.*

MR. FOWLER. Did I hear you say something about a telephone call?

MISS COOPER. I'm afraid it wasn't from your guest, Mr. Fowler. It was from Major Pollock. He wanted to leave a new forwarding address.

MRS RAILTON-BELL. Ringing up from London? That's very extravagant – for the Major –

MISS COOPER (*with a faint smile*). He was calling from a friend's house, I gather. He's coming back next Tuesday he says.

MISS MEACHAM (*through her book*). Oh God! That old bore!

MR. FOWLER. I can't understand Philip not ringing up. How can he expect to be met at the station if we don't know what train –

MISS COOPER. Have you tried ringing him?

MR. FOWLER. Yes. Twice. No answer either time. Perhaps I'd better try again –

He goes through the change in his pocket.

MISS COOPER. It's a little late, Mr. Fowler. There's only one train left from London –

MR. FOWLER (*on his way to the door*). Please don't worry about the room, Miss Cooper. If anything's gone wrong – which I don't believe, mind you – I'll pay for it, I promise you.

MISS COOPER. That won't be necessary, Mr. Fowler. But I *would* rather like to know – if you don't mind – as soon as possible –

MR. FOWLER *goes.* MISS COOPER *takes up the vase from his table.*

MRS. RAILTON-BELL (*sympathetically*). It's too bad, Miss Cooper. This is the third time, isn't it?

MISS COOPER. I expect he'll turn up. Just forgotten to phone, that's all. You know what these Bohemian young people are like.

She goes out.

MRS. RAILTON-BELL (*to* LADY MATHESON). I don't as it happens. I don't care for Bohemians. (*In her confidential whisper.*) We have one too many here, I should have thought. (*With her head she indicates the table by the window.*) And I'm beginning to doubt the very existence of Mr. Fowler's famous young painter friend.

LADY MATHESON. I know he exists. Mr. Fowler showed me an article on him in *Picture Post*. He was the head boy of Mr. Fowler's house at Tonbridge, I gather. So proud of him, Mr. Fowler is – it's really quite touching to hear him go on –

MRS. RAILTON-BELL. Well, I think it's a disgrace that he keeps on letting him down like this –

MISS MEACHAM *suddenly closes her book.*

MISS MEACHAM. Nonsense.

MRS. RAILTON-BELL (*startled*). What, dear?

MISS MEACHAM. It's not a disgrace at all. Why should we old has-beens expect the young to show us consideration? We've had our life. They've still got theirs to live. Seeing us can only remind them of death, and old people's diseases. I've got two of the prettiest nieces you ever saw. You've seen their photographs in my room. But they never come near me, and I wouldn't like it if they did. God knows I don't want to remind them of what they've got to become.

She goes into the lounge, holding her book.

MRS. RAILTON-BELL (*in her confidential whisper to* LADY MATHESON). I'm getting a little worried about Miss Meacham.

LADY MATHESON. She's certainly getting more and more unusual, every day.

MRS. RAILTON-BELL. These dream-games of hers. Well, I suppose they're harmless – but I really don't know what a psychiatrist would say. The human mind, you know – it's a very delicate piece of machinery – as my husband used to say – and – one never knows. Well – (*She rises majestically.*) Shall I see you in the lounge, or have you a date with the Third Programme?

LADY MATHESON. No. There's nothing worth hearing on tonight.

MRS. RAILTON-BELL. Good. A toute à l'heure, then.

She sweeps regally into the lounge. LADY MATHESON *is now on her sweet.* ANNE *has finished toying with her goulash. Deep silence reigns.* MABEL *comes in.*

MABEL (*to* ANNE). I've brought you the turnover. It's better than the other.

ANNE. Oh. Thank you so much.

MABEL *replaces her dishes and goes out. Once more
silence reigns. The door is pushed open rather violently, and
JOHN MALCOLM comes in. He is in the early forties, of
rather rugged appearance, untidily dressed, and with unruly
hair. When he speaks it will be with a slight north country
accent. He looks quickly, at his watch, and then at the
kitchen door. Then he walks towards the table by the window.
To reach it he has to pass ANNE. She has seen him before he
sees her, and is now staring at him remotely, with no change
of expression. Conscious of the stare he looks in her
direction and then stops dead, his back to the audience. After
a moment he walks on to his own table and takes his seat,
which is facing hers. He stares at the table-cloth. DOREEN
comes in.*

DOREEN. Oh. You in at last? Thank heavens. I thought we'd
never get off. Where you been? The Feathers?

JOHN. Yes.

DOREEN. Thought so. The goulash's off. You'll have to have
medaillon.

JOHN (*still staring at the table-cloth*). That's all right.

DOREEN. Brown windsor, like usual?

JOHN. Yes.

DOREEN *goes. There is silence between the three. Finally
LADY MATHESON finishes, gets up, and goes out into the
lounge, as DOREEN comes in with JOHN's soup.*

DOREEN. There you are. Tuck into that. Not but what I
wouldn't expect you've had enough liquid tonight already.

She goes out. JOHN *crumbles a piece of bread, and then
slowly lifts his eyes from the table-cloth to gaze at the other
guest.*

JOHN (*at length*). Is this coincidence?

ANNE. Of course.

JOHN. What are you doing here?

ANNE. A rest-cure.

JOHN. Why this place – of all places?

ANNE. It was recommended to me.

JOHN. Who by?

ANNE. A man I met at a party somewhere.

JOHN. He didn't tell you I was here?

ANNE. He did say something about a journalist – called John
Malcolm. Is that you?

JOHN. Yes.

ANNE. John Malcolm. Oh yes, of course. Your Christian
names.

JOHN (*savagely*). Why, for the love of God, didn't you go to
the Royal Bath or the Norfolk or the Branksome Towers, or
any of the grand hotels – why?

He stops as DOREEN *comes in.*

DOREEN. What you having after, 'cause cook's got to leave
it out? Turnover is best.

JOHN. All right.

DOREEN. Finished your soup?

JOHN. Yes, thank you.

DOREEN. You haven't touched it. I *said* too much liquid –

She takes the soup into the kitchen.

ANNE. I couldn't afford a grand hotel.

JOHN. He pays you alimony, doesn't he?

ANNE. Seven fifty a year. I don't find it very easy. You see, I'm
not getting work these days –

JOHN. I thought he was a rich man.

ANNE. Michael? Oh no. His antique shop lost a lot of money.

JOHN. He gets his name in the papers a lot.

ANNE. Oh yes. Quite a social figure – first nights and all that.

JOHN. How long exactly were you married to him?

ANNE. Three years and six months.

JOHN. Beating me by three months? I saw the headlines of the case. They were quite juicy – but not as juicy as ours – you'll admit. It was cruelty again, wasn't it?

ANNE. Yes.

JOHN. Did *he* try to kill you too?

ANNE (*quietly*). No.

> DOREEN *comes in with* JOHN*'s second course.*

DOREEN. There you are. Usual veg? (JOHN *nods.* DOREEN *helps him.*) You look a bit down in the dumps tonight. Anything the matter?

JOHN. No.

DOREEN. All right. Don't take long, will you? My friend's waiting –

She goes out. JOHN *makes no attempt to touch his food.*

JOHN. How did he show *his* cruelty?

ANNE. In a lot of ways. Small ways. They can all be summed up by saying that he doesn't really like women.

JOHN. Why did he marry you?

ANNE. He wanted a wife.

JOHN. And you wanted a husband? (*She nods.*) As wide a contrast as possible from your first, I suppose. Still, couldn't you have done a bit better for yourself?

ANNE. I suppose so. But he was gentle and kind and made me laugh and I was fond of him. I went into it with my eyes well open. I thought I could make it work. I was wrong. (JOHN *laughs suddenly.*) What's the joke?

JOHN. A nice poser for a woman's magazine. Girls, which husband would you choose? One who loves you too little –

or one who loves you too much? (*After a pause*.) Third time lucky perhaps.

ANNE. Perhaps.

Pause.

JOHN. How long are you staying here?

ANNE. I booked for two weeks.

JOHN. I'll go to London.

ANNE. No. If you feel like that, then I'll go to another hotel.

JOHN. That might be easier.

Pause.

ANNE. John – I don't see why –

JOHN. Do you think these old women don't notice anything? They spend their whole days gossiping. It would take them less than a day to nose out the whole story and wouldn't they have a time with it! They're suspicious enough of me as it is. They know I write in the *New Outlook* under the name of Cato – and how they found that out I'll never know, because none of them would sully their dainty fingers by even touching such a bolshie rag.

ANNE. I read it every week.

JOHN. Turning left-wing in your old age?

ANNE (*quietly*). My old age?

JOHN. How old are you now?

ANNE. Well – let's just say eight years older than when I last saw you.

JOHN. Yes. You don't look it.

ANNE. Thank you. But I feel it.

Pause.

JOHN. Why didn't you come to see me in prison yourself?

ANNE. I wanted to. I was stopped.

JOHN. Who by?

ANNE. My mother and father.

JOHN. I suppose they told you I might try to strangle you in front of the warder. I nearly did try to strangle your solicitor.

ANNE. They thought it would make it easier for you if I kept away.

JOHN. A very well-bred, Christian thought. My dear ex-in-laws. How are they?

ANNE. My father's dead. My mother lives in a place rather like this, in Kensington.

Pause. JOHN is gazing at her intently.

JOHN (*at length*). Then you'll go tomorrow, will you?

ANNE. Yes.

JOHN. Thank you. (*Stiffly.*) I'm sorry to have to put you to so much inconvenience.

ANNE. That's all right.

He gets up abruptly from his table and walks up to hers. ANNE rises quickly.

JOHN. Well, what do we do – shake hands?

ANNE. I'm very glad to see you again, John.

She kisses him gently on the cheek.

JOHN. It may seem boorish of me not to be able to say the same, Anne. But then I am a boor, as you know. In fact, you must still have a scar on the side of your head to prove it to you.

ANNE. It's gone now.

JOHN. Gone? After five stitches and a week in hospital?

ANNE. Eight years will cure most scars.

JOHN. Most, I suppose. Not all, though. Well, good night.

He goes towards the hall door. Before he reaches it MISS
COOPER *comes in.*

MISS COOPER. Mrs. Shankland – (*Seeing* JOHN.) Oh, good
evening, Mr. Malcolm.

JOHN. Good evening.

He makes to move past her.

MISS COOPER. Did you want something? Is there anything
I can do for you?

JOHN. I've finished, thank you. I'm going out.

MISS COOPER. Oh. (*With a hint of anxiety.*) It's a horrible
night, you know. It's started to pour –

JOHN. It doesn't matter –

He goes into the hall.

MISS COOPER (*following him*). I'll have to open the door for
you. I've already locked up. Excuse me, Mrs. Shankland –

She follows him out. ANNE, *left alone, sits down again. She
looks thoughtfully at herself in a hand-mirror for a long
time.* MISS COOPER *comes back.*

Coffee is served in the lounge, Mrs. Shankland. I thought
when you've finished your dinner, you might like me to take
you in there and introduce you to some of your fellow-
guests. People are sometimes so odd about not talking to
newcomers, I don't know why, and I hate any of my guests
to feel lonely. (*Conversationally.*) Loneliness is a terrible
thing, don't you agree?

ANNE. Yes, I do agree. A terrible thing.

She gets up from the table.

MISS COOPER. Oh. Have you finished? Good. Then let's go
in, shall we? The lounge is through here.

She leads the way to the lounge door.

ANNE. Thank you.

The lights fade.

Scene Two

Scene: the lounge, about two hours later. The dining-room door is upstage right and the door leading to the hall is at back. French windows, left, are curtained and we can hear the rain beating against them. There is a fireplace downstage right with an electric fire burning.

CHARLES *and* JEAN *are the only two residents in the room. They sit side by side on a sofa, still reading intently. Both are making an occasional note.*

CHARLES (*breaking a long silence, into his book*). There's going to be a storm.

JEAN. Hell. I hate spray.

CHARLES (*after another silence*). Where are they all ?

JEAN. The new one's gone up to her room. So has old Dream-girl. The Bournemouth Belle and Minnie Mouse are in the television room. Karl Marx is out boozing. Mr. Chips is still ringing up his painter friend.

CHARLES. He won't come.

JEAN. Of course he won't. (*She closes her book and stretches herself.*) I've finished my Stubbs. How are you doing with your anatomy?

CHARLES. I'd do better if you'd shut up.

JEAN (*going to the window*). I didn't start the small talk. You did. Does your father know about me?

CHARLES (*making a note*). Yes.

JEAN. What did you tell him?

CHARLES. What?

She pushes his book against his lap, preventing him from reading.

JEAN. What did you tell him?

CHARLES. Don't do that, Jean. I'm in the middle of the trickiest duct in the whole human body.

JEAN. What did you tell him?

CHARLES (*angrily*). Oh, for God's sake – that we were in love with each other and were going to get married.

He pulls the book back and furrows his brows over it again.

JEAN. You told him a dirty lie, then, didn't you – I mean about us going to get married?

CHARLES. What? Oh yes. I had to put it like that. Otherwise he wouldn't have understood. Now shut up for God's sake.

JEAN. You'd better stop now. If you go on much longer you know you won't sleep and it'll make you old before your time.

He allows her to take the book from him.

CHARLES. I suppose you're right. Don't lose the place. (*He stretches.*) My God – to be old before one's time. What a fate! I wonder if all old people are as miserable as these.

JEAN. They're not miserable. Look at old Dream-girl. She's as happy as a sandgirl communing with her spirits and waiting for the racing results. The Bournemouth Belle's quite happy, too, queening it around here in her silver fox, and with her daughter to look after her.

CHARLES. Has she got a daughter?

JEAN. Don't you listen to anything? She never stops trilling away about her dear Sibyl, and how they're really more like good pals than mother and daughter, and how dear Sibyl can't live without her –

CHARLES. You mean the daughter lives with her here? My God, what a fate! I haven't seen her –

JEAN. She's escaped for a couple of weeks, I gather, to an aunt. Anyway, the Bournemouth Belle's too self-centred an old brute to be anything but happy. Minnie Mouse *is* a bit grey and depressed, I grant. But she's got her music, and Mr. Chips has got his ex-pupils, even if he doesn't ever see them. As for Karl Marx – well –

CHARLES. Now you can't say Karl Marx isn't miserable. I've never seen a more miserable-looking wreck –

JEAN. Oh, I don't know. He's got his booze and his articles in the *New Outlook* and his vague air of a murky past, and his hints of former glories. (*With seriousness.*) No, Charles. Do you know who I think is the only one in this hotel who really *is* miserable?

CHARLES. Miss Cooper?

JEAN (*scornfully*). Miss Cooper? No. She's as gay as a bee pinning up her notices in the bathroom and being generally managerial. No. I meant the new one.

CHARLES. Mrs. Shankland? But you've only met her for a second an hour ago.

JEAN. A woman can't fool another woman with a pretty dress and a gay manner and a bright smile. She's been through some form of hell, that creature. Anyway, what's she doing down here? Dressed like that and looking like that she ought to be at the Royal Bath, or somewhere – (*Darkly.*) Besides – she's not wearing a wedding ring.

CHARLES. Really, Jean, you're getting as bad as the old girls. Perhaps it's got broken or something.

JEAN. She's divorced – that I'm sure of.

CHARLES. Well, all right. So she's divorced. Does that make her a tragic figure? I should have thought according to your ideas on marriage, it ought to make her a happy one.

JEAN. My ideas on marriage are only for us, Charles – because I'm going to have a career and you're going to be a famous surgeon and don't want hordes of children cluttering up your consulting-room. But most people aren't as sensible as we are. They get married and are miserable when it goes wrong. Thank heavens that can't happen to us. We're too integrated. At least I am, I know, and I hope you are too –

CHARLES. Come and give me a kiss and I'll show you how integrated I am.

JEAN. I'd only put lipstick on your collar and the old girls will notice.

CHARLES. Sometimes, Jean darling, I'm not sure I wouldn't like to see you, just ever so slightly, disintegrate.

He strides over and kisses her. She appears quite to enjoy the embrace. There is the sound of voices in the hall.

CHARLES. Oh blast!

JEAN (*levelly*). Wipe your mouth.

CHARLES. Damn it all, even the old girls know the facts of life.

JEAN. They may know them, but they don't like them.

MRS. RAILTON-BELL *and* LADY MATHESON *come in.*

MRS. RAILTON-BELL. Yes, wasn't he splendid? He completely floored that horrid socialist – (*Coldly.*) Hullo. Finished your work?

CHARLES. Yes.

JEAN (*overlapping*). Yes we have. Just going to bed.

MRS. RAILTON-BELL. Good night.

CHARLES. Good night, Mrs. Railton-Bell.

JEAN (*overlapping*). Good night, Lady Matheson.

They go out.

MRS. RAILTON-BELL. They've been making love.

LADY MATHESON. How do you know?

MRS. RAILTON-BELL. The look in their eyes. And just as I came in he was putting a handkerchief away with lipstick marks on it.

LADY MATHESON. Well, perhaps they *are* in love. I always thought there must be something.

MRS. RAILTON-BELL. But they're supposed to have come here just to work. Old friends, and all that. That's what they told Miss Cooper. If they're in love, why don't they say so? I hate anything furtive. What were we saying?

They take their (evidently usual) seats by the fire.

LADY MATHESON. About the man on television being so good.

MRS. RAILTON-BELL. Oh yes. Now what was it he said that was so true –

The french windows are opened from the outside and the curtains are blown violently inwards.

Good gracious!

After a moment's battling with the bellying curtains, JOHN *emerges. He is wearing a drenched raincoat.*

Please close that at once. There's the most terrible draught.

JOHN. A draught? Oh yes.

He disappears behind the curtains again. MRS. RAILTON-BELL *exchanges a speaking glance with* LADY MATHESON *and frames the word 'drunk' with her lips.*

LADY MATHESON. Yes. Now what was it he said? So telling. Something about the national cake.

JOHN*'s struggles to close the french windows are concluded. He emerges again and, still in his mackintosh, walks over to a chair by the fire, where he warms his hands. The two ladies look at him, and* MRS. RAILTON-BELL *decides to ignore his presence.*

MRS. RAILTON-BELL. Yes. I remember now. It was in that wonderful answer he gave about levelling up rather than levelling down. He said, don't you remember, that whereas the Socialists were only concerned about cutting the national cake into exactly equal slices, the Conservatives were trying to increase the size of the cake.

She glances at JOHN *to see if this has registered. Still holding his hands to the fire he does not appear to have heard.*

MRS. RAILTON-BELL. And then he said that every wage increase meant a smaller cake for cutting –

JOHN (*abruptly*). Who said this?

MRS. RAILTON-BELL. Sir Roger Williamson, on television.

JOHN. I might have guessed it.

MRS. RAILTON-BELL (*bristling*). I gather you don't agree with what he said, Mr. Malcolm?

JOHN. Of course I don't agree. You know damn well I don't agree. That's not the point. They've got some clever people in that party. Why do they have to put an old ass like that on television – with a falsetto voice, a face like an angry walrus and the mind of a backward child of eight?

MRS. RAILTON-BELL. That was *not our* impression of Sir Roger.

JOHN *does not reply. He seems, for the moment, to be lost in reverie.*

JOHN. Poor old Roger. I suppose he needs the dough to make a little back on what he spends on all those girl friends of his.

MRS. RAILTON-BELL (*after a moment's appalled silence*). Do I understand that you are personally acquainted with Sir Roger, Mr. Malcolm?

JOHN *turns and looks at her as if, for the moment, he had been oblivious of her presence.*

JOHN. No. Never met him.

MRS. RAILTON-BELL. Then may I ask by what right –

JOHN. No right. I just hear things, that's all.

MRS. RAILTON-BELL. Some very libellous things, if I may say so.

JOHN. Yes, the greater the truth the greater the libel is the phrase, isn't it? What else did Sir Roger say? Did he mention the go-slow in the docks?

MRS. RAILTON-BELL. Yes. As a matter of fact he did. He said that the dock workers seemed to have no sense of national responsibility –

JOHN. There's no body of men in England with more.

MRS. RAILTON-BELL. That's no doubt something else that you have *heard*, Mr. Malcolm.

JOHN. No. That's something I *know*, I used to be a docker myself.

Pause.

MRS. RAILTON-BELL (*at length*). I am not, if I may say so, at all surprised to hear it.

JOHN. And I am not surprised you're not surprised, Mrs. Railton-Bell. (*He burps gently.*) Excuse me. Too much whisky.

He sits down, still in his mackintosh. MRS. RAILTON-BELL *and* LADY MATHESON *exchange a glance,* JOHN *intercepts it.*

Keeps the cold out, you know. I gather you two ladies read the *New Outlook?*

MRS. RAILTON-BELL. I certainly never do any such thing. I wouldn't soil my hands –

JOHN. That's just what I thought. Do you, Lady Matheson?

LADY MATHESON. I have glanced at it on occasions, yes. (*Hastily.*) Not for the political side, of course, but it has very good music criticism.

JOHN. So it was you who found out I was Cato, was it? Smart of you. How did you guess?

LADY MATHESON (*confused*). If you must know, you left some typescript lying about on that table over there. I picked it up, not knowing what it was, and read just the opening paragraph, no more, but it was enough for me to recognize it in print a week or so later.

JOHN. I see. My fault then. No ill-feelings – on this side anyway. (*He burps again*.) Excuse me. What was the article on?

LADY MATHESON. Dividends and wages.

JOHN. Did you read it all?

LADY MATHESON. Yes, I did.

JOHN. What did you think of it?

LADY MATHESON (*with unusual spirit*). Since you ask I thought it was monstrous – utterly monstrous. I very nearly wrote you a letter about it.

JOHN. I wish you had. I enjoy controversy. You must have taken it a bit personally, I'm afraid.

LADY MATHESON. And how else could I take it? Do you realise that I have to live on a little less than half of what the average dock worker makes a year? My husband was in the Civil Service and died before the pension scheme came into force. Still, the sum he left me seemed perfectly adequate at the time. And now –

JOHN. I know. You can't afford to have your wireless repaired – and you live by it. You had to move into a small back room when they raised the hotel prices last year. You can only afford one cinema a week, in the front rows. I bet you don't even buy the *New Outlook* – you borrow it. In short by any reasonable standards you're well below the poverty line, and, as the poor have always had my passionate sympathy, Lady Matheson, you have mine.

LADY MATHESON. Thank you, but I can do very well without it.

JOHN. I wonder if you can. You're the unlucky victims of our revolution – you and Miss Meacham and Mr. Fowler and the others. You should appeal to our humane instincts, Lady Matheson.

LADY MATHESON. By voting for your side, I suppose.

JOHN. That would be the most practical way, I agree.

LADY MATHESON (*staunchly*). Never. Never till I die.

MRS. RAILTON-BELL. Tell me, why didn't you mention *me* just now, when you were talking of victims?

JOHN. Because you're not one, and won't be, either, until our capital levy gets at that tidy little nest-egg of yours.

MRS. RAILTON-BELL (*utterly outraged. To* LADY MATHESON). I think we should go, Gladys, and leave Mr. Malcolm down here to sleep it off.

The two ladies rise.

JOHN. Oh, are you leaving, ladies? I mustn't forget my manners, must I?

He gets out of the chair, with slight difficulty.

I've enjoyed our little chat. Don't forget, next election – vote Labour.

MRS. RAILTON-BELL. It's our own fault, Gladys. We should never have allowed ourselves to be drawn into an argument with a drunken red.

She has plainly intended this as an exit line, but her exit is delayed because LADY MATHESON *is feverishly searching the room for something.*

(*Impatiently.*) Come along, Gladys.

LADY MATHESON. I've left my reading glasses somewhere.

MISS COOPER *comes in with a tray on which is a coffee-pot and a cup.*

MISS COOPER (*brightly*). Here you are, Mrs. Railton-Bell. I'm not too late, I hope.

MRS. RAILTON-BELL (*with heavy meaning*). Thank you, Miss Cooper, but I'm not having my coffee tonight. (*Impatiently, to* LADY MATHESON.) Can't you find them, dear?

LADY MATHESON. I'll just have another look in my chair.

She goes to her chair. MISS COOPER *meanwhile has quickly taken in the scene. She puts the tray down and she stares coldly at* JOHN.

MISS COOPER (*in a very managerial voice*). Mr. Malcolm, did you come in through the french windows?

JOHN (*humbly*). Yes, I did.

MISS COOPER. You know that there's a hotel rule against that?

JOHN. I'd forgotten it. I'm very sorry.

MISS COOPER. There's mud all over the floor, (*advancing on his chair*) and you've been sitting in this chair with your wet mackintosh on. Oh really!

JOHN. I'm very sorry.

MISS COOPER. I must ask you if you would be so kind as to take your mackintosh off and hang it up in the proper place. Also to wipe your shoes on the mat provided for that purpose.

JOHN. Yes. I'm very sorry.

He goes past MRS. RAILTON-BELL *and out into the hall.* LADY MATHESON *is still looking in her chair.*

MISS COOPER (*anxiously*). Has there been a little bother?

MRS. RAILTON-BELL. A little bother is a distinct under-statement.

MISS COOPER. Oh dear! What was it?

MRS. RAILTON-BELL. I would prefer not to discuss it now. (*Very impatiently.*) For heaven's sake come along, Gladys. That dreadful man may be back at any moment.

LADY MATHESON (*triumphantly*). Ah, I've got them. They were underneath the chair.

MRS. RAILTON-BELL. I can't think why you didn't look there in the first place.

LADY MATHESON. Well, I was sitting in Mr. Fowler's chair after dinner, you see, as the new lady was sitting in mine, quite inadvertently, I'm sure, and I thought –

MRS. RAILTON-BELL. It doesn't matter, dear. Go along now. Quick.

She shoos her through the door and turns to MISS COOPER.

I should like to see you tomorrow morning after breakfast, Miss Cooper. Good night.

MISS COOPER. Good night, Mrs. Railton-Bell.

MRS. RAILTON-BELL *goes out.* MISS COOPER *sighs and goes over to the chair in which* JOHN *has sat. She takes the cushion out and places it near the fire.* MR. FOWLER *comes in, and goes over to the writing-desk.*

MR. FOWLER. Ah, there you are, Miss Cooper. I've come for some notepaper.

MISS COOPER. Any luck, Mr. Fowler?

MR. FOWLER. I'm afraid not. I shall try again, of course. I'm quite sure there's been some mistake – a telegram wrongly addressed, or something.

MISS COOPER. I expect so.

MR. FOWLER. I don't want anyone to wait up, but as I can hear the front-door bell from my room, I wonder if you'd mind if I answer it myself tonight?

MISS COOPER. That's quite all right, Mr. Fowler, but you're surely not still expecting him, are you?

MR. FOWLER. He might have hired a car, you know. He's a very extravagant boy. You know what these artists are. Well, good night.

MISS COOPER. Good night, Mr. Fowler.

MR. FOWLER *goes out.* MISS COOPER *wanders over to inspect the muddy footprints on the carpet. She is on her knees as* JOHN *comes back. He sits down moodily, in silence.* MISS COOPER *methodically finishes scraping up pieces of dried mud, walks to the waste-paper basket and throws them in. Then she goes to* MRS. RAILTON-BELL*'s unwanted coffee and pours a cup, black, with two lumps of sugar. Silently she hands it to him. He takes it, looking up at her, and sips it. She sits on the arm of his chair and leans her head affectionately on his shoulder.*

(*Gently.*) Are you very drunk?

JOHN. No.

MISS COOPER. How many?

JOHN. As many as I could afford. It wasn't a lot.

Pause. She takes his hand.

MISS COOPER. Something's the matter, isn't it?

JOHN. Nothing much.

MISS COOPER. Want to tell me?

JOHN. I can't tell you.

MISS COOPER (*cheerfully*). That's all right. What did you say to the old women?

JOHN. Too much. Far too damn much. Oh God!

He puts the coffee down, gets up and walks away from her. She watches him anxiously.

I may have to leave.

MISS COOPER (*sharply*). You can't leave.

JOHN. I may have to.

MISS COOPER. You won't have to. I'll see to that. But was it so bad?

JOHN (*bitterly*). Not very bad, I suppose. Just an ordinary show-off, a rather sordid little piece of alcoholic self-assertion. Taking it out on two old women, telling them what a brilliant political thinker I am, hinting at what a great man I once was. I even gave away that I used to work in the docks.

MISS COOPER. Oh Lord!

JOHN. And that I knew Roger Williamson. I think I covered
that up, though. I hope I did.

MISS COOPER. I hope you did too, otherwise old Railton-Bell
will be on to it like a bloodhound. Anything else?

JOHN. I don't know. I can't think now. I'll remember it all in
the morning. (*Miserably.*) Oh, Pat. I'm so sorry.

He puts his arm round her affectionately.

MISS COOPER. That's all right. I'll cover up for you. Finish
your coffee.

He obediently takes the cup up again.

JOHN. Why do I do these things? I used to know how to
behave.

MISS COOPER (*kissing him gently on the cheek*). I'd do them
too, in your place.

JOHN. Don't over-dramatise me. I do that enough myself. I'd
probably have been nothing.

MISS COOPER. What about that newspaper cutting about
yourself you showed me which prophesied – ?

JOHN. One political tipster napping an outsider. If nothing
happens his tip is forgotten. If, by a fluke, it does, he can say:
'Look how clever I was twenty years ago – '

MISS COOPER. But before you were even thirty you'd been
made a Junior Minister.

JOHN (*brusquely rising*). Yes, yes, yes. It doesn't matter.
The world is full of promising young men who haven't, in
middle age, fulfilled their promise. There's nothing to that.
Nothing at all.

He has turned away from her and is staring at the floor.

MISS COOPER (*quietly*). I wish you'd tell me what's
happened.

JOHN. I can't. I've told you I can't. But it's not important.

MISS COOPER. Important enough for quite a few whiskies.

JOHN. A lot of things are important enough for that. The day I heard Willy Barker had been made a Cabinet Minister I had a bottle.

Pause.

MISS COOPER. Couldn't you *ever* get back?

JOHN *laughs sharply.*

JOHN. God, what a field day for the Tory press that would be! John Malcolm Ramsden has decided to stand as a Labour Independent for his old constituency. It will be recalled that Mr. Ramsden, who was a Junior Minister in the 1945 Administration, went to prison for six months in 1946 on the triple charge of assaulting a police officer in the course of his duty, of being drunk and disorderly and of causing grievous bodily harm to his wife. The headline – Gaol-Bird Stands Again. No thank you. I'll stay John Malcolm – journalist, middle-aged soak and has-been, the terror of the older lady residents of the Hotel Beauregard, Bournemouth. That's vastly preferable, I assure you.

He has turned away from her again. She goes up to him quietly and puts her arms on his shoulders.

MISS COOPER. John, dear, I don't want to know what it is, but let me help you, if I can.

He turns round and gazes at her.

JOHN (*simply*). Do you know, Pat, that I love you very sincerely?

MISS COOPER (*with a smile*). Sincerely? That sounds a little like what a brother says to a sister.

JOHN (*with an answering smile*). You have surely reason enough to know that my feelings for you can transcend the fraternal.

MISS COOPER. Yes. But for all that – and don't think I'm not grateful for all that – not really quite enough reason.

*They are drawing together when there is a sound outside the
hall door and they move apart, not in alarm, and as if from
long practice.* ANNE *comes in.*

MISS COOPER (*brightly*). Oh, hullo, Mrs. Shankland. They
told me you'd gone up some time ago.

ANNE. I had, but not to bed. I was reading.

MISS COOPER. That's a comfy armchair, in there, isn't it?

ANNE. Very.

She stands, uncertainly, just inside the door, looking at
JOHN *who, after a brief glance, has turned slightly away
from her.*

MISS COOPER. Was there anything you wanted, Mrs.
Shankland?

ANNE (*diffidently*). No. I just wanted a word or two with –
Mr. Malcolm.

MISS COOPER (*brightly, again*). Oh really? Had you two met
before ?

ANNE. Yes. A long time ago.

MISS COOPER. Oh.

She glances at JOHN, *evidently disturbed at the danger to
his anonymity inherent in this situation, but she gets no
answering look.*

Oh well. I'll leave you two alone, then. If you want anything,
I shall be up for quite a time yet.

She goes out, closing the door. ANNE *gazes steadily at her
ex-husband, but he is still looking away from her.*

ANNE. I didn't want to go away without our saying something
to each other, John. I hope you don't mind?

JOHN. Mind? Why should I mind?

ANNE. Your rushing out of dinner like a whirlwind made it
look as if you hated the very sight of me.

JOHN (*slowly, looking at her fully for the first time*). The very sight of you, Anne, is perhaps the one thing about you that I don't hate.

ANNE (*with a slight, nervous laugh*). Oh dear. That's not very nice to hear.

JOHN. Don't you enjoy being complimented on your looks any more? Has your narcissism vanished?

ANNE. No. I suppose not. But I don't enjoy being hated by you.

JOHN. Don't you? You used to.

ANNE. You've got me wrong, John. You always did, you know.

JOHN (*quietly*). I don't think so, Anne. If I had I wouldn't have found you so predictable.

ANNE. You always used to say I was predictable. I remember that was one of the things that used to irritate me most. It's such an easy thing to say, and so impossible to disprove.

JOHN. Yes, yes, yes. I've no doubt. Go to bed, Anne, and disappear quietly tomorrow. It's better, really it is.

ANNE. No, John. Let me stay just a little longer. May I sit down?

JOHN. Is that a way of reminding me of my bad manners? I know I shouldn't sit while you're standing –

ANNE (*laughing gently*). You're so bristly. Even bristlier now than before. (*She sits down.*) Your manners were always very good.

JOHN. You used to tick me off about them often enough.

ANNE. Well – only sometimes – when we had silly conventional people at the flat who didn't understand you as I did.

JOHN (*with a faint smile*). I think if I'd been given time, I could have predicted that answer.

ANNE (*with an answering smile*). Oh dear! Tell me, did you always find me so predictable – even at the very beginning?

JOHN. Yes.

ANNE. Why did you marry me, then?

JOHN. If it pleases your vanity to hear my answer once again, you shall. Because my love for you at that time was so desperate, my craving for you was so violent, that I could refuse you nothing that you asked – not even a marriage that every prompting of reason told me must be disastrous.

ANNE. Why did it so necessarily have to be disastrous?

JOHN. Because of class mainly.

ANNE. Class? Oh, that's nonsense, John. It's just inverted snobbery.

JOHN. No. I don't think so. The gulf between Kensington Gore and the Hull Docks is still fairly wide. I was one of a family of eight, as I must have told you many a time, and my views of a wife's duties must have been at least a little coloured by watching my mother sacrifice her health, strength and comfort and eventually her life to looking after us children, and to keeping the old man out of trouble. I'm not saying my demands on a wife would have been pitched as high as that. But they would, I think, at least have included the proper running of a home and the begetting of children.

ANNE (*hotly*). About children, I did make it perfectly clear before our marriage –

JOHN. Yes. You made it perfectly clear. A famous model mustn't gamble her figure merely for posterity. I accepted the bargain, Anne, the whole bargain. I have no complaint.

ANNE (*angrily*). You have, John. You know you have. Your real complaint is still the same as it always was – that I didn't love you when we got married –

JOHN. Oh God! Do we have to go into that again?

ANNE. Yes, we do, it needs clearing up. You admitted just now that I was the one who wanted the marriage. All right. If that's true – which it is – what could have been the motive, except love? Oh yes. I know. You were an under-secretary at the time, but, let's face it, there were even grander figures that I might have –

JOHN (*interrupting*). I know, Anne dear. I remember it all in detail. A baronet, an Australian millionaire, and that film producer.

ANNE. Well, then?

JOHN (*quietly*). You married me because you were frightened. You were going to be thirty. You'd realized suddenly that you couldn't go on for the rest of your life gazing joyously at yourself in the mirror, because the time would come when what you saw in the mirror would no longer give you joy. And you couldn't go on treading happily on the faces of all the men who wanted you, because the time would come when there wouldn't be so many faces to tread on.

ANNE. Eloquent, John, but unconvincing. If so, why not a baronet, or a millionaire? Why Mrs. Ramsden?

JOHN. Because the others couldn't pay you the full price.

ANNE. What price?

JOHN. The price you so reluctantly put on yourself when you settled for giving yourself to the highest bidder in marriage.

ANNE. You mean, a title wasn't enough?

JOHN. No.

ANNE. Nor a million?

JOHN. Nor a million.

ANNE. What was the price then?

JOHN. Enslavement.

ANNE. John, really. How ridiculous you are. I seem to remember this accusation from the old days –

JOHN. I've no doubt you do.

ANNE. If all I wanted to do was to make my husband a slave, why should I specially have chosen you and not the others?

JOHN. Because where would your fun have been in enslaving
the sort of man who was already the slave of his own head
gardener? You wanted bigger game. Wilder game. None of
your tame baronets and Australian millionaires, too well-
mannered to protest when you denied them their conjugal
rights, and too well-brought-up not to take your headaches at
bedtime as just headaches at bedtime. 'Poor old girl! Bad
show! So sorry. Better in the morning, I hope. Feeling a bit
tired myself, anyway.' No, Anne, dear. What enjoyment
would there have been for you in using your weapons on that
sort of a husband? But to turn them on a genuine, live,
roaring savage from the slums of Hull, to make him grovel at
the vague and distant promise of delights that were his
anyway by right, or goad him to such a frenzy of drink and
rage by a locked door that he'd kick it in and hit you with his
fist so hard that you'd knock yourself unconscious against a
wall – that must really have been fun.

ANNE (*at length*). Goodness, John, how you do go on.

JOHN. Yes. I do. You must forgive me. It's a foible, perhaps, of
disappointed politicians. Besides, tonight I'm rather drunker
than usual.

ANNE (*with a hint of eagerness*). Because of seeing me?

JOHN. Yes.

ANNE. I'm sorry.

JOHN. No you're not.

ANNE *laughs, quite gaily now, and with far more confidence.*

ANNE. You haven't changed much, have you?

JOHN. Haven't I?

ANNE. The same old John pouring out the same old cascade of
truths, half-truths and distortions, all beaten up together, to
make a neat, consistent story. *Your* story. Human nature isn't
quite as simple as you make it, John. You've left out the most
important fact of all.

JOHN. What's that?

ANNE. That you're the only person in the world I've ever been really fond of. You notice how tactfully I leave out the word love. Give me a cigarette. (*He pulls a packet from his pocket.*) Oh, not *still* those awful cork-tipped things. I'll have one of my own. Hand me my bag.

A faint note of authority has crept back into her voice. JOHN *obediently hands her her bag and she takes out a gold cigarette-case.*

Do you dispute that?

JOHN. I might observe that your fondness for me was sometimes shown in rather surprising ways –

ANNE. Well, I wasn't prepared to be your doormat. I had to fight back sometimes, didn't I?

JOHN. I suppose so. It was your choice of weapons that was unfair.

ANNE. I didn't have any others. You had the brains and the eloquence and the ability to make me feel cheap – which, incidentally, you've done again tonight.

JOHN. Have I? I'm sorry.

ANNE. Anyway, isn't it a principle of war that you always play on the opponent's weakness?

JOHN. A principle of war, not necessarily of marriage.

ANNE. Marriage is a kind of war.

JOHN. It is for you.

ANNE (*with a smile*). For you too, John. Be fair now.

JOHN. And the weakness you played on was my overpowering love for you?

ANNE. You can put it that way, if you like. There are less pretty-sounding ways.

JOHN *remains silent, looking at her as she smokes her cigarette, through a holder – now plainly quite confident of herself.*

Besides you and I never could have agreed on *that* aspect of married life.

JOHN. No. We couldn't.

ANNE. Why are you staring at me?

JOHN. You know very well why.

ANNE (*contentedly*). Well, don't. It makes me embarrassed.

JOHN. I'm sorry.

ANNE. You really think I haven't changed much – to look at, I mean?

JOHN (*not looking at her*). Not at all.

ANNE. Just a clever make-up, I expect.

JOHN. I don't think so.

ANNE. If you'd wanted an obedient little hausfrau, why didn't you marry one – like that manageress I caught you canoodling with a moment ago? That *was* a canoodle, wasn't it?

JOHN. A canoodle is what you would call it – yes.

ANNE. Why haven't you married her?

JOHN. Because I'm not in love with her.

ANNE. Does that matter?

JOHN. I'm old-fashioned enough to think it does.

ANNE. Couldn't you – as they say – *learn* to love her? After all she's your type.

JOHN. I have still only one type in the whole world, Anne. God knows it does little for my pride to have to admit that to you, but I never was very good at lying about myself. (*Looking at her again.*) Only one type. The prototype.

ANNE (*quietly*). I'm glad.

JOHN. I've no doubt you are. Tell me, does a compliment still give you that little jab in the solar plexus that you used to describe to me?

ANNE. Yes, it does. More so than ever, now that I'm forty.
There – I've admitted it.

JOHN. I'd worked it out anyway.

They both laugh quietly. He picks up her cigarette-case.

That's a nice little affair. Who gave you that? Your second?

ANNE. Yes.

JOHN. He had good taste.

ANNE. In jewels.

JOHN. You ought to have made a go of it with that man. He
sounds much more your form.

ANNE. He wasn't a man. He was a mouse.

JOHN. Didn't he pay you enough compliments?

ANNE. Too many and none of them meant.

JOHN. No solar plexus?

ANNE. No.

She takes his hand suddenly in an intimate friendly gesture.

John, I'm in a bad way, you know.

JOHN. I'm sorry.

ANNE. Some of the things you used to tell me might happen to
me *are* happening.

JOHN. Such as?

ANNE. Loneliness – for one.

JOHN. No friends?

ANNE. Not many. I haven't the gift.

JOHN. There's no gift. To make people love you is a gift, and
you have it –

ANNE. Had it –

JOHN. Have it.

ANNE. Yet I hate being alone. Oh God, how I hate it. This place, for instance, gives me the creeps,

JOHN (*innocently*). Why did you come here, then?

For the briefest instant she looks startled, but recovers at once.

ANNE. I suppose I didn't realize what it would be like. Oh God! What a life. I can just see myself in a few years' time at one of those separate tables –

JOHN. Is there no one on the horizon?

ANNE. No one that I'd want. And time is slipping. God, it goes fast, doesn't it?

JOHN. I haven't found it to, these last eight years.

ANNE. Poor John. I'm so sorry. (*She squeezes his hand.*) But it's such a wonderful fluke our meeting again like this, that we really shouldn't waste it. We must see some more of each other now. After all when fate plays as astounding a trick as this on us, it must mean something, mustn't it? Don't send me away tomorrow. Let me stay on a little while.

JOHN *makes no reply. He is staring at her.*

(*Gently.*) I won't be a nuisance.

JOHN *still does not answer. He is still staring at her.*

I won't, John. Really I won't.

JOHN (*at length murmuring thickly*). You won't be a nuisance.

He embraces her suddenly and violently. She responds. After a moment she begins to say something.

(*Savagely.*) Don't speak. For God's sake, don't speak. You'll kill this moment.

ANNE. Darling John, even at the risk of 'killing your moment' I think I really *must* say something. I think I must remind you that we are in a public lounge, and inform you that Miss Cooper has been good enough to give me what appears to be a very isolated room, the number of which is – (*she pulls a key from her pocket)* – nineteen. Give me one of those horrid cork-tipped things of yours. I'm right out of mine.

He takes a packet and brusquely thrusts them at her. She takes a cigarette. He tenders a lighter to her. His hand is trembling.

Oh – what a shaky hand!

She holds it still and lights her cigarette. JOHN *thrusts his hand back into his coat pocket and keeps it there. She gets up, gathers her bag in silence, smooths her dress, makes some adjustment to her hair, and turns to him.*

How do I look? All right?

JOHN (*murmuring*). All right.

ANNE (*happily blowing him a kiss*). Darling John.

JOHN (*not returning the gesture*). Darling Anne.

ANNE. Half an hour?

She goes towards the door. Before she gets there MISS COOPER *can be heard calling* 'Mrs. Shankland' *from the hall.* ANNE *stops and smiles at* JOHN.

ANNE. You see?

The door opens and MISS COOPER *comes in.*

MISS COOPER. Oh, Mrs. Shankland – you're wanted on the telephone – a London call.

ANNE. Oh? Where is the telephone?

MISS COOPER. I'll show you. It's just through here.

The two women go out. Left alone JOHN *sits down suddenly, as if his knees had weakened. He rests his head on his hands. He is in that attitude when* MISS COOPER *comes back. She looks at him for a moment before she speaks.*

That's her, isn't it?

JOHN. What?

MISS COOPER. Mrs. Shankland. That's the one, isn't it?

JOHN. Yes.

MISS COOPER. She looks exactly the way you described her. Carved in ice, you said once, I remember.

JOHN. Did I?

MISS COOPER. What's going to happen now, John?

He looks up at her without replying. There is a pause.

(*Quietly, at length.*) I see. Well – I always knew you were still in love with her and always would be. You never made any bones about that –

JOHN (*pleadingly*). Pat, dearest –

MISS COOPER. No. You don't need to say anything. I understand. So you'll be going away, will you?

JOHN. I don't know. Oh God, I don't know.

MISS COOPER. I expect you will. She looks as if she'd got some will-power, that girl. If she's taken that much trouble to run you to earth down here, she won't let you go so easily –

JOHN. She hasn't run me to earth. It was a coincidence her coming down here.

MISS COOPER. Coincidence? Do you really believe that?

JOHN. Yes.

MISS COOPER. All right, then. I'm not saying anything.

JOHN. Say it.

MISS COOPER. No, I won't.

He jumps up and fiercely, grabs her by the arms.

JOHN (*fiercely*). Say it. Say it, damn you.

MISS COOPER (*quietly*). Don't knock *me* about, John. I'm not her, you know.

He relaxes his grip.

MISS COOPER. All right. I'll say it. If it was coincidence, why is she talking to the editor of the *New Outlook* on the telephone now?

JOHN. What?

MISS COOPER. His name's Wilder, isn't it?

JOHN. Yes.

MISS COOPER. Terminus number?

JOHN. Yes.

MISS COOPER. And he knows who you really are, doesn't he, and where you live?

JOHN. Yes.

MISS COOPER. And he goes around the West End quite a bit, I'd imagine – cocktail parties and things?

JOHN *has sat down again, this time without replying.*

Mind you, it could be a different Mr. Wilder, I suppose. If there's one coincidence – why not another?

ANNE *comes back. She looks happy and unruffled.*

ANNE (*to* MISS COOPER). Thank you so much, Miss Cooper. I'm going to bed now. I've put down a call for 8.30 with hot water and lemon. I hope that's all right?

MISS COOPER. Quite all right, Mrs. Shankland.

ANNE. Well, good night. Good night, Mr. Malcolm.

JOHN *gets up suddenly from his chair.*

JOHN. Stay here, Anne. Pat, you go.

MISS COOPER (*urgently*). Not now, John. Leave it till the morning.

JOHN. It's got to be now.

He holds the door open for her.

Leave us alone, Pat, please.

MISS COOPER *goes out quietly.* JOHN *closes the door after her and turns to face* ANNE.

When fate plays as astounding a trick as this it must mean something, Anne, mustn't it?

ANNE. Yes, that's what I said.

JOHN (*harshly*). What did you tell Wilder?

ANNE *opens her mouth to speak.*

No, no. There's no need to lie any more. I'll quote you, shall I? My dear, our little plot's gone off quite wonderfully. Thank you so much for your help. Ten minutes alone with him was all I needed to have him grovelling. My dear, it was too funny, but after only one kiss his hand was shaking so much he couldn't even light my cigarette. You should have seen it. You'd have died laughing. Oh yes. He's at my feet again, all right, and I can tread on his face just any time I like from now on.

He has advanced on her slowly, and stands facing her. She stands her ground, but looks a little scared.

ANNE (*sincerely*). John, please, don't be so angry with me. It's not as if I'd done anything so terrible. I had to see you again. I was desperate to see you again, and this was the only way I could think of –

JOHN. The only way *you* could think of, of course. You wouldn't have thought of writing me a letter, or ringing me up, or telling me the truth in there? (*He points to the dining-room.*) Oh no. You had to have your conquest, you had to have your unconditional surrender, and if you could do it by lying and cheating so much the better. It makes the greater triumph.

ANNE. That's not true. Really it isn't. Oh yes, I should have told you, John. Of course I should have told you, but you see even now I've still got a little pride left –

JOHN. And so have I, Anne, thank God. So have I.

He puts his hands on her arms and pulls her close to him, staring at her face.

Yes, I can see the make-up now all right. Yes, Anne, I can see little lines there that weren't there before and it won't be very long now before this face will begin to decay and then there'll be nothing left to drive a man to –

He has slipped his hands on to her throat.

ANNE (*quietly*). Why don't you?

He stands looking down at her for a moment and then pushes her violently away. She falls from the chair on which she has been sitting, and in her fall knocks over an occasional table. JOHN goes to the french windows, pulls them open, and runs out. The wind blows the curtains into the room. She gets up from the floor and stands quite still, her face expressionless. There is a mirror over the fireplace and she stares at herself for a long time. She turns quickly away, and begins to sob, quietly at first, and then more violently until, as she makes her way blindly to the hall door, it is uncontrollable. MISS COOPER comes in before ANNE has reached the door. ANNE, seeing her barring the way, runs back into the room, still sobbing. MISS COOPER deliberately closes the windows, before turning to ANNE. Then she approaches her and puts her hand on her shoulder.

MISS COOPER. Come to my room, won't you, Mrs. Shankland? There's a fire there and a nice comfortable chair and I've even got a little sherry, I think. We'll be quite cosy there and no one can disturb us.

She begins to move her towards the door.

You see, someone might come in here and we don't want that, do we? Come along now, Mrs. Shankland. Come along –

She is leading her towards the door as

The lights fade.

Scene Three

Scene: the dining-room, the following morning. MISS
MEACHAM *sits at her table, poring over the sporting page of
a morning paper. The two undergraduates are at their table
reading. The other tables have been occupied, except for the
table by the window, and* ANNE*'s.* MISS COOPER *comes in
from the lounge.*

MISS COOPER (*talking into the lounge*). Yes, Mrs. Railton-
Bell, I promise I will.

The murmur of MRS. RAILTON-BELL*'s voice can be heard
off.*

Yes, utterly disgraceful, I quite agree. I shall speak to him
most severely.

She closes the door with a faint sigh.

(*Brightly, to the two undergraduates.*) Good morning, Miss
Tanner. Good morning, Mr. Stratton.

*They reply with a polite murmur and plunge back into their
books.*

Good morning, Miss Meacham. It looks as if we're going to
have a nice dry day at last.

MISS MEACHAM. Is it going to be dry at Newbury? – that's
the point. Walled Garden's a dog on heavy going.

MISS COOPER. Ah, now there you have me, Miss Meacham.

MABEL *comes in.*

MABEL. Miss Cooper, Mr. Malcolm wasn't in his room when I
took his tea up, and his bed hadn't been slept in.

MISS COOPER (*with a reassuring smile*). Yes, I know, Mabel.

MABEL. You know?

MISS COOPER. I should have told you, of course, but I'm afraid I clean forgot. He had to go to London unexpectedly last night.

MABEL. He won't be in to breakfast, then?

MISS COOPER. I don't suppose so.

The undergraduates go into the lounge.

MABEL. That's something anyway. It's nearly ten, now. What about the new lady? She's not down yet.

MISS COOPER. Yes, she's down, Mabel, but I don't think she's having breakfast.

MABEL. Not having breakfast?

MISS COOPER. She has to be very careful of her figure, you see.

MABEL (*with puzzled gloom*). Can't see what good a figure's going to be to you, when you're dead of starvation.

She goes into the kitchen.

MISS MEACHAM. She's leaving, isn't she, the new one?

MISS COOPER. Yes. She is, how did you know?

MISS MEACHAM. I heard her ask for her bags to be brought down. I knew she'd never stick it.

MISS COOPER (*coldly*). *Stick* it, Miss Meacham?

MISS MEACHAM. Oh, I don't mean the hotel. Best for the price in Bournemouth. I've always said so. I meant the life. All this – (*She indicates the empty tables.*) – She's not an 'alone' type.

MISS COOPER. Is any type an 'alone' type, Miss Meacham?

MISS MEACHAM. Oh yes. They're rare, of course, but *you* are for one, I'd say.

MISS COOPER. Am I?

MISS MEACHAM. Oh, I'm not saying you won't fall in love one day, and get married, or something silly like that. I'm only saying that if you don't you'll be all right. You're self-sufficient.

MISS COOPER (*a shade wearily, but polite*). I'm glad you think so, Miss Meacham. Perhaps even a little gladder than you realize.

MISS MEACHAM. What do you mean by that?

MISS COOPER. I've no idea. I'm a bit tired this morning. I had very little sleep last night.

MISS MEACHAM. Well – I don't suppose you *are* glad, really. Probably you haven't had to face up to it yet. I faced up to it very early on – long before I was an old wreck – while I was still young and pretty and had money and position and could choose from quite a few. (*Reminiscently.*) Quite a few. Well, I didn't choose any of them, and I've never regretted it – not for an instant. People have always scared me a bit, you see. They're so complicated. I suppose that's why I prefer the dead ones. Any trouble from them and you switch them off like a television set.

She rises.

No, what I've always said is – being alone, that's the real blessed state – if you've the character for it. Not Mrs. What's-her-name from Mayfair, though. I could tell that at a glance. A couple of weeks here and she'd have her head in the gas oven. It's pork for lunch, isn't it?

MISS COOPER. Yes, Miss Meacham.

MISS MEACHAM. I loathe pork. Ah well. I'd have a bit on Walled Garden, dear, if I were you. He's past the post if the going's on top.

She goes out. MISS COOPER, *left alone, slumps wearily into the chair* MISS MEACHAM *has vacated. She washes out* MISS MEACHAM*'s cup and pours some coffee out for herself. She sips it, and then lets her head fall wearily forward on to her chest, in an attitude of utter exhaustion.*

After a moment JOHN *comes in slowly from the hall. After a look round he walks up to her quietly.*

JOHN (*in a low voice*). Pat. I must see you a moment.

MISS COOPER *opens her eyes and looks up at him. She jumps to her feet as she takes him in.*

MISS COOPER. Are you all right?

JOHN. Yes. I'm all right.

MISS COOPER. Where did you go?

JOHN. I don't know. I walked a long way.

MISS COOPER. Were you out all night?

JOHN. No. I sat in a shelter for a time. Pat, I've got to have some money. I'm broke to the wide. I spent my whole week's cheque in the Feathers last night –

MISS COOPER. How much do you want?

JOHN. Enough to get me on a train and keep me some place for a few days. Three, or four pounds, I suppose. Can you let me have it, Pat?

MISS COOPER. You won't need it, John. She's going.

JOHN. Are you sure?

MISS COOPER. Yes.

JOHN. Where is she now?

MISS COOPER. In my office. It's all right. She won't come in here.

She feels his clothes.

Did you get very wet?

JOHN. Yes, I suppose so. It's dried off now.

MISS COOPER. You'd better sit down and have some breakfast. Your hands are like ice. (*She rings a bell.*)

JOHN. I don't want anything to eat. Just some tea.

MISS COOPER. All right. Now sit down. Straighten your tie a bit, and turn your collar down. That's better. Now you look quite respectable.

She pulls out a chair for JOHN *to sit down at his table.* DOREEN *comes in.*

DOREEN. Yes, miss? (*Seeing* JOHN.) Oh, you back? I suppose you think you can have breakfast at this time?

MISS COOPER. Just some tea, Doreen – that's all.

DOREEN. Okey doke.

She goes into the kitchen.

MISS COOPER. She'll have to go, that girl. (*She turns to* JOHN.) Well, that was a fine way to behave, dashing out into the night, and scaring us out of our wits –

JOHN. Us?

MISS COOPER. Oh yes. She was scared too. I stopped her from calling the police.

JOHN. So you talked, did you?

MISS COOPER. Most of the night. She was a bit hysterical and needed quieting. I didn't want to get a doctor.

JOHN. Did I – Pat, tell me the truth – did I hurt her?

MISS COOPER. Her throat? No.

JOHN. She fell though, didn't she? I seem to remember pushing her, and her falling and hitting her head – or perhaps I'm confusing it with –

MISS COOPER (*firmly*). She's as right as rain. There isn't a mark on her of any kind.

JOHN (*murmuring*). Thank God.

DOREEN *comes in with a pot of tea and a plate.*

DOREEN. I brought you some digestive biscuits. I know you like them.

JOHN. Thank you. Thank you, Doreen, very much.

DOREEN. Had a tumble or something? You've got mud all over your arm.

JOHN. What? Oh yes. So I have. Yes, I remember now. I fell down last night in the dark.

DOREEN. Give it to me after and I'll get it off.

She goes out.

MISS COOPER. I should have seen that. I'm sorry.

JOHN. It's all right. They'll just think I was drunk. How is she this morning?

MISS COOPER. A bit shaky. Quieter, though. Did you know she took drugs?

JOHN. Drugs? What sort of drugs?

MISS COOPER. Oh, just those things that make you sleep. Only she takes about three times the proper dose and takes them in the day too.

JOHN. How long has this been going on?

MISS COOPER. About a year, I gather.

JOHN. The damn little fool. Why does she do it?

MISS COOPER (*shrugging*). Why do you go to the Feathers?

Pause.

Yes – there's not all that much to choose between you, I'd say. When you're together you slash each other to pieces, and when you're apart you slash yourselves to pieces. All told, it's quite a problem.

Pause.

JOHN. Why didn't she tell me about this last night?

MISS COOPER. Because she's what she is, that's why. If she'd shown you she was unhappy she'd have had to show you how much she needed you and that she'd never do – not her – not in a million years. Of course that's why she lied about coming down here. I've got rather a bad conscience about that, you know, I should never have told you. Just a flash of jealousy, I suppose. I'm sorry.

JOHN. What time is she leaving?

MISS COOPER. She's only waiting now to get some news of you. I was just going to start ringing up the hospitals. She asked me to do that.

JOHN. I see. Well, when I've finished this I'll slip out somewhere. You can tell her that I'm all right. Then when she's gone you can give me a ring.

MISS COOPER. You don't think you might tell her that yourself ?

Pause.

JOHN. No.

MISS COOPER. It's your business, of course, but I think if I were in your place, I'd want to.

JOHN (*savagely*). You don't know what it's like to be in my place. You can't even guess.

MISS COOPER (*quietly*). I think I can. Gosh, I'm tired. I shouldn't be sitting here gossiping with you. I've got work to do. You'd better let me tell her you're here.

JOHN. No, Pat, don't. Give me one good reason why I should ever see her again. Just one reason –

MISS COOPER. All right. Just one then. And God knows it's not for me to say it. Because you love her and because she needs your help.

Pause.

JOHN (*suspiciously*). What went on between you two last night? How did she win you over?

MISS COOPER. She didn't win me over, for heaven's sake. Feeling the way I do, do you think she could? Anyway, to do her justice she didn't even try. She didn't give me an act and I could see her as she is, all right. I think all you've ever told me about her is probably true. She *is* vain and

spoiled and selfish and deceitful. Of course, with you being
in love with her, you look at all those faults like in a kind of
distorting mirror, so that they seem like monstrous sins and
drive you to – well – the sort of thing that happened last
night. Well, I just see them as ordinary human faults, that's
all – the sort of faults a lot of people have – mostly women,
I grant, but some men too. I don't like them but they don't
stop me feeling sorry for a woman who's unhappy and
desperate and ill and needing help more than anyone I have
ever known. Well? Shall I call her in?

JOHN. No. Pat. No. Don't interfere in this. Just let her go back
to London and her own life, and leave me to live the rest of
mine in peace.

MISS COOPER (*quietly*). That'd be fine, John, if you'd just tell
me a little something first. Exactly what kind of peace *are*
you living in down here?

JOHN. A kind of peace, anyway.

MISS COOPER. Is it? Is it even really living?

He makes no reply.

Is it, John? Be honest, now. Oh, I know there's your work
and your pals at the Feathers and – well – me – but is it even
living?

Pause.

JOHN (*shortly, at length*). It'll do.

MISS COOPER (*with a faint laugh*). Thank you. I'm glad you
didn't hand me one of those tactful tarradiddles. I *did* try –
you know – when we first began – you and I – all that time
ago – I *did* try to help you to get back into some sort of life.
As a matter of fact I tried very hard –

JOHN. I know you did.

MISS COOPER. It didn't take me long, though, to see I hadn't
a hope.

JOHN. Don't blame me for that, Pat. Circumstances, as they
say, outside my control –

MISS COOPER. Outside your control? Yes. That's right. (*Quite brightly.*) When you think of it it seems really rather a pity you two ever met, doesn't it?

JOHN. Yes. A great pity.

MISS COOPER (*brightly*). If you hadn't, she'd have been a millionairess, and you'd have been Prime Minister, and I'd have married Mr. Hopkins from the bank, and then we'd have all been happy. I'm going into my office now and I'm going to tell her you're here. I'll have a word with Mr. Fowler first, about a room he didn't take up, so if you want to skedaddle, you can. The door's through there and the street's outside, and down the street is the Feathers. It is a bit early, but I've no doubt they'll open for you.

She goes into the lounge.

(*As she goes.*) Oh, Mr. Fowler, I'm so sorry to bother you, but I just want to have a word –

The door closes behind her. Left alone JOHN *stands in evident doubt and irresolution. Then he sits down at his table.* DOREEN *comes in.*

DOREEN. Have you finished?

JOHN. Not quite, Doreen.

DOREEN. Make up your mind.

She begins to clear some things from the other tables. ANNE *comes in from the lounge.* JOHN *doesn't look at her.*

Oh, hullo, Mrs. Shankland. You're a bit late for breakfast, I'm afraid. I expect you didn't know. There's some coffee left, though, or tea if you'd rather, and I can get you some biscuits. Is that all right?

ANNE. Thank you. That's very kind. Coffee please. Not tea.

DOREEN. Righty-oh.

She goes into the kitchen.

ANNE (*standing by* JOHN's *table, pleadingly*). John. (*He doesn't look up.*) John –

JOHN (*quietly*). You'd better sit at your table. She'll be back in a moment.

ANNE. Yes. Yes, I will.

She sits down at her table. He remains at his.

I was desperately worried about you.

JOHN. You needn't have been. I was quite all right. How are you now?

ANNE. All right too. (*After a pause.*) I'm going this morning, you know.

JOHN. So I heard.

ANNE. I won't bother you again. Ever again. I just wanted to say I'm sorry I had to lie to you –

JOHN. Thank you, Anne.

ANNE. I don't know why I did. Not for the reasons you gave, I think, though they may be right too, I admit. I don't seem to know very much about myself any more. I'm sorry, John.

JOHN. That's all right.

ANNE. I *am* an awful liar. I always have been – ever since school. I don't know why but I'd rather lie than tell the truth even about the simplest things. (*With a wan smile.*) It was nearly always about my lying that we used to quarrel in the old days – do you remember?

JOHN. Yes. I remember.

ANNE *lowers her head quickly as the tears come suddenly.*

ANNE. Oh, John. I don't know what's going to happen to me –

DOREEN *comes in with a tray.* ANNE *turns her head quickly away from her.* DOREEN *goes to* JOHN's *table first, and puts down a plate of biscuits.*

DOREEN. Thought you might like some more. I know your appetite.

She goes to ANNE's *table with some biscuits.* ANNE *has managed to wipe her eyes unseen.*

DOREEN. Here you are, Mrs. Shankland.

ANNE. Thank you.

DOREEN. Coffee's just coming.

DOREEN *goes out, having noticed nothing.*

ANNE (*smiling again*). Narrow escape. I'm sorry. I'm in a rather weak state this morning.

JOHN. How much money exactly does Shankland give you, Anne?

ANNE. I've told you – seven fifty. (*She meets his eyes. At length, murmuring shamefacedly.*) Fifteen hundred.

JOHN. Can't you live quite happily on that?

ANNE. How can *I* live happily on anything now?

JOHN. But you don't need to be alone in London. You may not have many friends, but you have hundreds of acquaintances, and surely you can go out and enjoy yourself –

ANNE. You can be more alone in London than in this place, John. Here at least you can talk from table to table. In London it's the phone and usually no answer.

Pause.

JOHN. You must give up those drugs. Anne.

ANNE. She told you ?

JOHN. They won't help, you know.

ANNE. I know they won't.

JOHN. Throw them all into the dustbin. They're no good, those things.

ANNE. I won't do that. I can't. I'm not strong enough. But I'll cut them down if I can.

JOHN. Try.

ANNE. I *will* try. I promise.

Pause.

JOHN. Tell me, Anne. When you say you need me, is it me you really mean, or just my love? Because if it's my love you must know now that you have that. You have that for life.

ANNE. It's you, John.

JOHN. But why? Why, for heaven's sake?

ANNE. I suppose because you're all the things I'm not. You're honest and true and sincere and dependable and – (*She breaks off and tries to smile.*) Oh dear, this is just becoming a boring catalogue of your virtues. Too embarrassing. I'm sorry, and that damn waitress will come in and catch me crying again.

JOHN (*slowly*). I may have had some of those virtues once, Anne. I'm not at all sure that I have them now, so I don't know if I'd be able to satisfy your need. I do know though that you can never satisfy mine.

ANNE. How can you know?

JOHN. Experience.

ANNE. Supposing I'd learnt something from the last eight years?

JOHN. It's not a lesson that can be learnt.

ANNE. I could still try.

JOHN. So could I, Anne. So could I. And we'd both fail.

ANNE. How can you be so sure?

JOHN. Because our two needs for each other are like two chemicals that are harmless by themselves, but when brought together in a test-tube can make an explosive as deadly as dynamite.

ANNE (*shrugging*). I could take the risk. After all, there are worse deaths, aren't there? (*She looks round the room at the empty tables.*) Slower and more painful and more frightening. So frightening, John. So frightening. (*She lowers her head as once more the tears come.*) I'm an awful coward you see. I never have been able to face anything alone – the blitzes in the war, being ill, having operations, all that. And now I can't even face – just getting old.

JOHN *gets up quietly from his table and walks to hers. She has her head lowered and a handkerchief to her eyes, so that it is only when she has recovered herself a little that she finds him sitting there. She looks at him without saying anything. He takes her hand.*

JOHN (*gently*). You realize, don't you, that we haven't very much hope together?

ANNE *nods, and holds his hand tight in hers.*

ANNE. Have we all that much apart?

DOREEN *comes in with* ANNE's *coffee. They release their hands.*

DOREEN (*seeing them*). Oh. (*To* JOHN.) Do you want your tea over there?

JOHN. Yes, please.

She brings his cup over, and gives ANNE *her coffee.*

Thank you.

DOREEN. Do you two want to sit at the same table from now on? You can, if you like.

JOHN. Yes. I think we do.

DOREEN. Oh. I'll make up a double for you for lunch then. It's just so long as we know –

She goes into the kitchen. JOHN *once again takes* ANNE's *hand.*

Curtain.

TABLE NUMBER SEVEN

Characters
in order of speaking

JEAN STRATTON
CHARLES STRATTON
MAJOR POLLOCK
MR. FOWLER
MISS COOPER
MRS. RAILTON-BELL
MISS RAILTON-BELL
LADY MATHESON
MISS MEACHAM
MABEL
DOREEN

Scene One: Lounge. After Tea.
Scene Two: Dining-Room. Dinner.

Scene One

Scene: the lounge of the Beauregard Private Hotel. It is, perhaps, eighteen months or so since the events of the preceding play, but apart from a rearrangement of the chairs to accord with the summer season, and a set of new covers on those chairs, there has been little alteration. CHARLES STRATTON, *in flannels and sports-shirt, lies on the sofa, reading some large medical treatise. Through the french windows, which are open,* JEAN STRATTON (née JEAN TANNER) *appears pulling a pram.*

JEAN (*to the unseen baby*). Tum along now. Tum along. Tum and see Daddy – Daddy will give you a little tiss and then beddy-byes –

CHARLES*'s face shows his annoyance at the interruption to his studies.*

CHARLES. Bed-time, already?

JEAN. After six. How are you getting along?

CHARLES. Miles behind. Endless interruptions. It was idiotic to come back to this place. I should have remembered what it was like from the last time. We could have borrowed David's cottage –

JEAN. Nasty air in the Thames Valley. Not good for baby. Bournemouth air much better, (*To baby.*) isn't it, my little lammykins? He says, Yes Mummy, lovely air, lovely sun, makes baby teep like an ickle top –

CHARLES. He doesn't say anything of the sort. All he ever appears to say is 'goo'. I'm getting a bit worried.

JEAN. Don't be silly, darling. What do you expect him to do at five months? Quote T. S. Eliot?

CHARLES. I think all this 'tum along' stuff you smother him in is bad for him. It's very dangerous, too, you know. It can lead to arrested development later on –

JEAN (*complacently*). What nonsense you do talk.

She has now sat on the sofa beside him and kisses him fondly. He turns from the caress a trifle brusquely.

JEAN. Give me a proper kiss.

CHARLES (*murmuring*). A kiss, but not a tiss.

He kisses her with a little more warmth, then breaks off.

JEAN. Go on.

CHARLES. No.

JEAN. Why not?

CHARLES. It's too early.

JEAN. You're so horribly coarse-grained sometimes that I wonder why I love you so much. But I do, you know, that's the awful thing. I've been thinking all the afternoon how much I loved you. Funny how it seems sort of to have crept up on me like this. Did it creep up on you too, or did you lie in your teeth before we got married?

CHARLES. I lied in my teeth. Now take baby up to beddy-byes, dear, and leave Daddy to his worky-perky – or Daddy won't ever become a docky-wocky.

There is the sound of a loud jovial voice in the garden.

MAJOR POLLOCK (*off*). Hullo, 'ullo, Miss Meacham. Working out the form, eh? Got any tips for tomorrow?

MISS MEACHAM (*off*). Let me see.

CHARLES. Oh God! Here's the Major. Go on, darling, for heaven's sake. If he sees the baby we're lost. He'll talk for hours about infant welfare in Polynesia or something.

JEAN. All right. (*To baby.*) Tum along then – (*She meets* CHARLES*'s eyes. Firmly.*) Come along, then, Vincent Michael Charles. It is time for your bath and subsequently for your bed. Better?

MISS MEACHAM (*off*). Red Robin in the three-thirty.

CHARLES. Much.

He blows her a kiss as she goes out into the hall with the pram, from which emerges a faint wail.

JEAN (*as she goes*). Oh. Did Mummy bring him out of 'ovely garden into nasty dark pace. Naughty Mummy.

Her voice subsides. CHARLES *returns to his book.*

MAJOR POLLOCK (*off*). Red Robin in the three-thirty? I'll remember that. Not that I can afford much these days, you know. Not like the old days when one would ring up the hall porter at White's, and get him to put on a couple of ponies. Lovely day, what?

MISS MEACHAM (*off*). Not bad.

MAJOR POLLOCK comes in. He is in the middle fifties, with a clipped military moustache and extremely neat clothes. In fact both in dress and appearance he is almost too exact a replica of the retired major to be entirely true.

MAJOR POLLOCK. Hullo, Stratton. Still at it?

CHARLES (*with only the most perfunctory look-up from his book*). Yes, Major.

MAJOR POLLOCK. Don't know how you do it. Really don't. Most praiseworthy effort, I think.

CHARLES. Thank you, Major.

Pause. The MAJOR *sits.*

MAJOR POLLOCK. Of course when I was at Sandhurst – oh so sorry – mustn't disturb you, must I?

CHARLES (*politely, lowering his book*). That's all right, Major. When you were at Sandhurst?

MAJOR POLLOCK. Well, I was going to say that I was a bit like you. Off duty, while most of the other young fellers were gallivanting about in town, I used to be up in my room, or in the library there, cramming away like mad. Military history – great battles of the world – Clausewitz – that sort of stuff. I could have told you quite a lot about Clausewitz once.

CHARLES. Oh. And you can't now?

MAJOR POLLOCK. No. Afraid not. Everything goes, you know. Everything goes. Still I didn't regret all those hours of study at the time. I did jolly well at Sandhurst.

CHARLES. Did you get the Sword of Honour?

MAJOR POLLOCK. What? No. Came quite close to it, though. Passed out pretty high. Pretty high. Not that it did me much good later on – except that they made me battalion adjutant because I was good at paper work. Could have been brigade major, as it happens, Turned it down because I thought, if trouble came – well – you know – miles behind the line – away from one's own chaps. I suppose it was a bit foolish. I'd probably have been a general now, on full pay. Promotion was always a bit tight in the Black Watch. Should have chosen another regiment, I suppose.

CHARLES (*plainly hoping to terminate the conversation*). Yes.

MAJOR POLLOCK. Go on my boy. Go on. So sorry. I talk too much. That's usually the trouble with old retired majors, what.

CHARLES. Not at all, sir. But I *will* go on, if you don't mind. I've rather a lot to do.

There is a pause. CHARLES *continues reading. The* MAJOR *gets up and, taking infinite pains not to make a sound, tiptoes to a table where he picks up a magazine, and tiptoeing back, sits down again.* CHARLES *has plainly been aware of the* MAJOR'*s tactfully silent passage.* MR. FOWLER *comes through the french windows, holding a letter.*

MR. FOWLER. Oh, hullo, Major. I've just had the most charming letter –

MAJOR POLLOCK (*putting his fingers to his lips, and indicating* CHARLES). Sh!

CHARLES *gets up resignedly and goes to the door.*

Oh, I say. I do hope we're not driving you away.

CHARLES. No, that's quite all right. I can always concentrate much better in my room.

MAJOR POLLOCK. But you've got the baby up there, haven't you?

CHARLES. Yes, but it's a very quiet baby. It hasn't learnt to talk yet.

He goes out.

MAJOR POLLOCK. Well, Fowler, who's your letter from? An old flame ?

MR. FOWLER (*chuckling happily*). Old flame? I haven't got any old flames. I leave that to you galloping majors.

MAJOR POLLOCK. Well, I used to do all right once, I must say. In the regiment they used to call me Bucko Pollock. Regency buck – you see. Still, those days are past and gone. *Eheu fugaces, Postume, Postume.*

MR. FOWLER (*correcting his accent*). *Eheu fugaces, Postume, Postume.* Didn't they teach you the new pronunciation at Wellington?

MAJOR POLLOCK. No. The old.

MR. FOWLER. When were you there?

MAJOR POLLOCK. Now let's think. It must have been nineteen eighteen I went up –

MR. FOWLER. But they were using the new pronunciation then, I know. Our head classics master was an old Wellingtonian, and I remember distinctly his telling me –

MAJOR POLLOCK. Well, perhaps they did and I've forgotten it. Never was much of a hand at Greek.

MR. FOWLER (*shocked*). Latin. Horace.

MAJOR POLLOCK. Horace, of course. Stupid of me. (*Plainly changing the subject*.) Well, who *is* your letter from?

MR. FOWLER. It's a boy, who used to be in my house and I haven't heard from for well over ten years. Brilliant boy he was, and done very well since. I can't think how he knew I was down here. Very good of him, I must say.

MAJOR POLLOCK. What happened to that other ex-pupil of yours – the painter feller?

MR. FOWLER. Oh. I still read about him in the newspapers occasionally. But I'm afraid I don't get much personal news of him. We've – rather lost touch, lately.

MISS COOPER *comes in with a newspaper under her arm.*

MISS COOPER. Good afternoon, Major, we've managed to get your copy of the *West Hampshire Weekly News*.

MAJOR POLLOCK (*eagerly*). Good afternoon, Miss Cooper.

MISS COOPER (*handing him the newspaper*). Joe had to go to three places before he could find one.

MAJOR POLLOCK. Thank you very much.

MISS COOPER. What was the urgency?

MAJOR POLLOCK. Oh – I just wanted to have a look at it, you know. I've never read it – strange to say – although I've been here – what is it – four years?

MISS COOPER. I'm not surprised. There's never anything in it except parking offences and cattle shows.

The MAJOR *opens the paper, turning away from her.*

MAJOR POLLOCK. Well, thanks anyway.

MR. FOWLER. I've had a charming letter, Miss Cooper, from someone I haven't seen or heard from in over ten years.

MISS COOPER (*brightly*). How nice. I'm so glad.

MR. FOWLER. I'm going to write to him and ask him if he'd care to come down for a day or two. Of course he probably won't – but just in case he does, will that room be vacant?

MISS COOPER. Not at the moment, I'm afraid, Mr. Fowler. We have so many casuals. But at the end of September –

MR. FOWLER. Good. I'll ask him for then.

During this interchange between MISS COOPER *and* MR. FOWLER, MAJOR POLLOCK, *unseen by them, has turned the pages of his paper over quickly, as if he was searching for something. Suddenly his eye is evidently caught by what he reads, and he folds the paper back with a sharp sound.* MR. FOWLER *looks up at him.*

MR. FOWLER. You were with the Highland Division at Alamein, weren't you, Major?

There is no immediate reply. When the MAJOR *does look up his eyes are glassy and staring.*

MAJOR POLLOCK. *What?* No. No I wasn't. Not with the Highland Division.

MR. FOWLER. I thought you were.

MAJOR POLLOCK (*almost fiercely*). I never said so.

MR. FOWLER. I just wondered because this boy – Macleod his name is – James, I think, or John – anyway he was known at school as Curly – he says in this letter he was with the Highland Division. I just wondered if you'd run into him at all.

MAJOR POLLOCK. Macleod? No. No, I don't think so.

MR. FOWLER. Well, of course, it would have been very unlikely if you had. It was just possible, though.

He goes to the door. MISS COOPER *has been straightening cushions and tidying up.* MAJOR POLLOCK *sits down, holding his paper, and staring blankly into space.*

(*To himself.*) Curly Macleod. He once elided a whole word in his Greek Iambics –

He chuckles to himself and goes out. MAJOR POLLOCK *looks down again at his paper, and, as* MISS COOPER *straightens herself from her labours, pretends to be reading it casually.*

MAJOR POLLOCK. Yes. Pretty dull, I grant you.

MISS COOPER. What?

MAJOR POLLOCK. This paper. I don't suppose it's much read, is it?

MISS COOPER. Only by locals, I suppose. Farmers, estate agents – those sort of people.

MAJOR POLLOCK. I've never heard of anyone in the hotel reading it – have you?

MISS COOPER. Oh yes. Mrs. Railton-Bell takes it every week.

MAJOR POLLOCK. Does she? Whatever for?

MISS COOPER. I don't know, I'm sure. There's not a lot that goes on in the world – even in West Hampshire – that she likes to miss. And she can afford fourpence for the information, I suppose.

MAJOR POLLOCK (*laughing jovially*). Yes, I suppose so. Funny, though – I've never seen her reading it.

MISS COOPER. Oh, she gets a lot of things sent in to her that she never reads. Most of the stuff on that table over there is hers –

MAJOR POLLOCK. Yes. Yes, I know. She'd have had hers this morning then, I suppose?

MISS COOPER. Yes. I suppose so.

MAJOR POLLOCK. Oh. Dash it all. Here I've gone and spent fourpence for nothing. I mean I could have borrowed hers, couldn't I?

He laughs heartily. MISS COOPER *smiles politely and having finished her tidying up, goes to the door.*

MISS COOPER. I know you don't like venison, Major, so I've ordered you a chop for lunch tomorrow. Only I must ask you to be discreet about it, if you don't mind.

MAJOR POLLOCK. Yes, of course. Of course. Thank you so much, Miss Cooper.

*MISS COOPER goes out. MAJOR POLLOCK opens the
paper quickly and stares at it for some time, reading avidly.
Then he suddenly rips out the whole page, crumpling it up
and thrusting it into his pocket. Then he goes quickly to the
table, and, after a feverish search. finds the 'West Hampshire
Weekly News'. He has turned it over to find the evidently
offending page when MRS. RAILTON-BELL walks into the
room from the hall, followed by her daughter SIBYL. The
latter is a timid-looking, wizened creature in the thirties,
bespectacled, dowdy and without make-up.*

MRS. RAILTON-BELL (*as she enters*). Well, if that's what you
meant, you should have said so, dear. I wish you'd learn to
express yourself a little bit better – Good afternoon, Major
Pollock.

MAJOR POLLOCK. Good afternoon, Mrs. Railton-Bell.
(*Jovially to* SIBYL.) Afternoon, Miss R.B.

*He is holding the paper, unable to hide it, or put it back
on the table. He sees that MRS. RAILTON-BELL has
noticed it.*

I'm so sorry. I was just glancing through your *West Hampshire News*. I wonder if you'd let me borrow it for a few
moments. There's something in it I want to see.

MRS. RAILTON-BELL. Very well, Major. Only please return
it.

MAJOR POLLOCK. Of course.

*He goes to the door. MRS. RAILTON-BELL has moved to
her seat. As she does so she picks up the other copy of the
'West Hampshire Weekly News' from the floor, where
MAJOR POLLOCK has dropped it.*

MRS. RAILTON-BELL. What's this? Here's another copy

MAJOR POLLOCK (*feigning astonishment*). Of the *West
Hampshire Weekly News?*

MRS. RAILTON-BELL. Yes.

MAJOR POLLOCK. Well I'm dashed.

MRS. RAILTON-BELL. It was on the floor over here.

MAJOR POLLOCK. Must be one of the casuals, I suppose.

MRS. RAILTON-BELL. You'd better take it, anyway, and leave me mine.

MAJOR POLLOCK (*doubtfully*). You don't think, whoever owns it, might –

MRS. RAILTON-BELL. If it's been thrown down on the floor, it's plainly been read. I'd like mine back, if you don't mind, please, Major.

MAJOR POLLOCK (*conceding defeat*). Righty-oh. I'll put it back with the others.

He does so, and takes the other copy from MRS. RAILTON-BELL.

Think I'll just go out for a little stroll.

SIBYL (*shyly*). You don't happen to want company, do you, Major Pollock? I haven't had my walk yet.

MAJOR POLLOCK (*embarrassed*). Well, Miss R.B. – jolly nice suggestion and all that – the only thing is I'm going to call on a friend – you see – and –

SIBYL (*more embarrassed than he*). Oh yes, yes. Of course. I'm so sorry.

MAJOR POLLOCK. No, no. I'm the one who's sorry. Well, cheerie-bye till dinner.

He goes out.

MRS. RAILTON-BELL. I wish he wouldn't use that revolting expression. It's so common. But then he *is* common –

SIBYL. Oh no, Mummy. Do you think so? He was in a very good regiment.

MRS. RAILTON-BELL. You can be in the Horse Guards and still be common, dear. (*Gently.*) Sibyl, my dearest, do you mind awfully if your tactless old mother whispers something in your ear?

SIBYL (*resigned*). No.

MRS. RAILTON-BELL. I didn't think it was *terribly* wise of you to lay yourself open to that snub just now.

SIBYL. It wasn't a snub, Mummy. I'm sure he really *was* going to see a friend –

MRS. RAILTON-BELL *smiles understandingly and sympathetically, shaking her head ever so slightly.*

Well, I often *do* go for walks with the Major.

MRS. RAILTON-BELL. I know you do, dear. What is more quite a lot of people have noticed it.

Pause. SIBYL *stares at her mother.*

SIBYL (*at length*). You don't mean – you can't mean – (*She jumps up and holds her cheeks with a sudden gesture.*) Oh no. How can people be so awful!

MRS. RAILTON-BELL. It's not being particularly awful when an unattached girl is noticed constantly seeking the company of an attractive older man.

SIBYL (*still holding her cheeks*). They think I chase him. Is that it? They think I run after him, they think I want – they think – no it *is* awful. It *is*. It *is*. It *is*.

MRS. RAILTON-BELL (*sharply*). Quieten yourself my dear. Don't get into one of your *states,* now.

SIBYL. It's all right, Mummy. I'm not in a state. It's just – well – it's just so dreadful that people should believe such a thing is even possible. I hate that side of life. I hate it.

MRS. RAILTON-BELL (*soothingly*). I know you do, dear. But it exists, all the same, and one has to be very careful in this world not to give people the wrong impression. Quieter now?

SIBYL. Yes, Mummy.

MRS. RAILTON-BELL. Good. You must try not to let these things upset you so much, dear.

SIBYL. I only go for walks with the Major because I like hearing him talk. I like all his stories about London and the war and the regiment – and – well – he's seen so much of life and I haven't –

MRS. RAILTON-BELL. I don't know what you mean by that, dear, I'm sure.

SIBYL. I only meant – (*She checks herself.*) I'm sorry.

MRS. RAILTON-BELL (*relentlessly pursuing her prey*). Of course I realize that you must occasionally miss some of the gaieties of life – the balls and the cocktail parties and things – that a few other lucky young people can enjoy. I can assure you, dearest, if I could possibly afford it, you'd have them. But I *do* do my best, you know.

SIBYL. I know you do, Mummy.

MRS. RAILTON-BELL. There was Rome last year, and our Scandinavian cruise the year before –

SIBYL. I know, Mummy. I know. Don't think I'm not grateful. Please. It's only – (*She stops.*)

MRS. RAILTON-BELL (*gently prompting*). Only what, dear?

SIBYL. If only I could *do* something. After all, I'm thirty-three –

MRS. RAILTON-BELL. Now, my dear. We've been over this so often. Dearest child, you'd never stand any job for more than a few weeks. Remember Jones & Jones?

SIBYL. But that was because I had to work in a basement, and I used to feel stifled and faint. But there must be something else.

MRS. RAILTON-BELL (*gently patting her hand*). You're not a very strong child, dear. You must get that into your head. Your nervous system isn't nearly as sound as it should be.

SIBYL. You mean my *states?* But I haven't had one of those for a long time –

MRS. RAILTON-BELL. No, dear – you've been doing very well. Very well, indeed. But there's quite a big difference between not having hysterical fits and being strong enough to take on a job. (*Concluding the topic decisively.*) Hand me that newspaper, would you, dear?

SIBYL. Which one?

MRS. RAILTON-BELL. The *West Hampshire Weekly News*. I want to see what the Major was so interested in.

SIBYL *hands her the paper.* MRS RAILTON-BELL *fumbles in her pockets.*

Oh, dear me, what a silly billy! I've gone and left my glasses and my book in the shelter at the end of Ragusa Road. Oh dear, I do hope they're not stolen. I expect they're bound to be. Now – doesn't that show how dependent I am on you, my dear? If you hadn't had that headache you'd have been with me this afternoon, and then you'd never have allowed me to –

SIBYL. I'll go and look for them.

MRS. RAILTON-BELL. Oh, would you, dear? That really is so kind of you. I hate you to fetch and carry for me, as you know – but my old legs are just a wee bit tired – it was the far end of the shelter, facing the sea.

SIBYL. Where we usually sit? I know.

She goes out. MRS. RAILTON-BELL *opens the paper and scanning it very close to her eyes, she turns the pages to what she plainly knows, from past experience, to be the interesting section. Suddenly she stops moving the paper across her eyes. We do not see her face but the paper itself begins to shake slightly as she reads.* LADY MATHESON *comes in.*

LADY MATHESON. Oh, hullo dear. It's nearly time for the newsreel.

MRS. RAILTON-BELL (*in a strained voice*). Gladys, have you got your glasses?

LADY MATHESON. Yes, I think so. (*She feels in her pocket.*) Yes, here they are.

MRS. RAILTON-BELL. Then read this out to me.

She hands her the paper and points.

LADY MATHESON (*unsuspecting*). Where, dear? Lorry
   driver loses licence ?

MRS. RAILTON-BELL. No, no. Ex-officer bound over.

LADY MATHESON (*brightly*). Oh yes. (*Reading.*) 'Ex-officer
   bound over. Offence in cinema.' (*Looking up.*) In cinema?
   Oh dear – do we really want to hear this?

MRS. RAILTON-BELL (*Grimly*). Yes, we do. Go on.

LADY MATHESON (*reading, resignedly*). 'On Thursday last,
   before the Bournemouth Magistrates, David Angus Pollock,
   55, giving his address as (*She starts violently.*) the Beauregard Hotel, Morgan Crescent – ' (*In a feverish whisper.*)
   Major Pollock? Oh!

MRS. RAILTON-BELL. Go on.

LADY MATHESON (*reading*). 'Morgan Crescent – pleaded
   guilty to a charge of insulting behaviour in a Bournemouth
   cinema.' Oh! Oh! 'On the complaint of a Mrs. Osborn, 43
   (*Breathlessly.*) of 4 Studland Road.' He must have been
   drinking –

MRS. RAILTON-BELL. He's a teetotaller.

LADY MATHESON. Perhaps just that one night.

MRS. RAILTON-BELL. No. Read on.

LADY MATHESON. 'Mrs. Osborn, giving evidence, stated that
   Pollock, sitting next to her, persistently nudged her in the
   arm, and later attempted to take other liberties. She
   subsequently vacated her seat, and complained to an
   usherette. Inspector Franklin, giving evidence, said that in
   response to a telephone call from the cinema manager,
   Pollock had been kept under observation by police officers
   from three fifty-three p.m. until seven-ten p.m. by which
   time he had been observed to change his seat no less than
   five times, always choosing a seat next to a female person.

There had, he admitted, been no further complaints, but that was not unusual in cases of this kind. On leaving the cinema Pollock was arrested and after being charged and cautioned stated: 'You have made a terrible mistake. You have the wrong man. I was only in the place half an hour. I am a colonel in the Scots Guards.' Later he made a statement. Appearing on behalf of the defendant, Mr. William Crowther, solicitor, stated that his client had had a momentary aberration. He was extremely sorry and ashamed of himself and would undertake never to behave in so stupid and improper a manner in future. He asked that his client's blameless record should be taken into account. He had enlisted in the army in 1925 and in 1939 was granted a commission as second lieutenant in the Royal Army Service Corps. During the war, he had held a responsible position in charge of an Army Supply Depot in the Orkney Islands, and had been discharged in 1946 with the rank of full lieutenant. Pollock was not called. The Chairman of the Bench, giving judgment, said: "You have behaved disgustingly, but because this appears to be your first offence we propose to deal leniently with you." The defendant was bound over for twelve months.'

She lowers the paper, disturbed and flustered to the core of her being.

Oh dear. Oh dear. Oh dear.

MRS. RAILTON-BELL (*perfectly composed but excited*). Thursday. It must have happened on Wednesday. Do you remember – he missed dinner that night?

LADY MATHESON. Did he? Yes, so he did. Oh dear. It's all too frightful! I can hardly believe it. Persistently. It's so dreadful.

MRS. RAILTON-BELL. On the Thursday he was terribly nervous and depressed. I remember now. And then on the Friday, suddenly as bright as a button. Of course he must have read the papers and thought he'd got away with it. What a stroke of luck that I get this weekly one sent to me.

LADY MATHESON. Luck, dear? Is it luck?

MRS. RAILTON-BELL. Of course it's luck. Otherwise we'd never have known.

LADY MATHESON. Wouldn't that have been better?

MRS. RAILTON-BELL. Gladys! What *are* you saying?

LADY MATHESON. I don't know, oh dear. I'm so fussed and confused. No, of course, it wouldn't have been better. One has to know these things, I suppose – although sometimes I wonder why.

MRS. RAILTON-BELL. Because if there's a liar and a fraudulent crook and a – I can't bring myself to say it – wandering around among us unsuspected, there could be – well – there could be the most terrible repercussions.

LADY MATHESON. Well, he's been wandering around among us for four years now and there haven't been any repercussions yet. (*With a faint sigh.*) I suppose we're too old.

MRS. RAILTON-BELL (*coldly*). I have a daughter, you know.

LADY MATHESON. Oh. Poor Sibyl. Yes. And she's such a friend of his, isn't she? Oh dear.

MRS. RAILTON-BELL. Exactly.

LADY MATHESON (*after a moment's troubled reflection*). Maud, dear – it's not my business, I know, and of course you have a mother's duty to protect your child, that of course I do see – and yet – well – she's such a strange girl – so excitable and shy – and so ungrownup in so many ways –

MRS. RAILTON-BELL. Come to the point, Gladys.

LADY MATHESON. Yes, I will. It's this. I don't think you ought to tell her this.

MRS. RAILTON-BELL. Not *tell* her?

LADY MATHESON. Well, not all of it. Not the details. Say he's a fraud, if you like, but not – please, Maud – not about the cinema. (*Suddenly distressed by the thought herself.*) Oh dear! I don't know how I shall ever look him in the face again.

MRS. RAILTON-BELL. You won't have to, dear. (*She has risen purposefully from her chair.*) I'm going to see Miss Cooper now, and insist that he leaves this hotel before dinner tonight.

LADY MATHESON. Oh dear. I wonder if you should?

MRS. RAILTON-BELL. Gladys, what *has* come over you this evening? Of course I should.

LADY MATHESON. But you know what Miss Cooper is – so independent and stubborn sometimes. She might not agree.

MRS. RAILTON-BELL. Of course she'll agree. She *has* to agree if we all insist.

LADY MATHESON. But we don't *all*. I mean it's just the two of us. Shouldn't we consult the others first? (*Suddenly realising the implication.*) Oh gracious! Of course that means we'll have to tell them all, doesn't it?

MRS. RAILTON-BELL (*delighted*). An excellent idea, Gladys. Where's Mr. Fowler?

LADY MATHESON. In his room, I think.

MRS. RAILTON-BELL. And the young people? Shall we have them? They count as regulars by now, I suppose. Yes. We'll have them too.

LADY MATHESON. Oh dear. I hate telling tales.

MRS. RAILTON-BELL. Telling tales? (*She points dramatically to the 'West Hampshire Weekly News'.*) The tale is told already, Gladys – to the world.

LADY MATHESON. Well, strictly speaking – only to West Hampshire.

MRS. RAILTON-BELL. Don't quibble, Gladys. (*At the french windows.*) Miss Meacham's in the garden. I really don't think we need bother about Miss Meacham. She's so odd and unpredictable – and getting odder and more unpredictable every day. Here comes Sibyl. Go up and get the others down, dear. I'll deal with her.

LADY MATHESON. Maud, you won't –

SIBYL *comes in.*

You'll remember what I said, won't you?

MRS. RAILTON-BELL. Yes, of course. Go on, dear.

LADY MATHESON *goes out.*

(*To* SIBYL.) Clever girl. You found them, did you, darling?

She takes the book and the glasses from SIBYL. *There is a pause.*

(*At length.*) Sibyl dear, I think you'd better go to your room if you don't mind.

SIBYL. Why, Mummy?

MRS. RAILTON-BELL. We're holding a meeting of the regulars down here to discuss a very urgent matter that has just cropped up.

SIBYL. Oh, but how exciting. Can't I stay? After all, I'm a regular, too –

MRS. RAILTON-BELL. I know, dear, but I doubt if the subject of the meeting is quite suitable for you.

SIBYL. Why, Mummy? What is it?

MRS. RAILTON-BELL. Oh dear! You're such an inquisitive child. Very well, then. I'll tell you this much – but only this much. We are going to discuss whether or not we think that Miss Cooper should be told to ask Major Pollock to leave this hotel at once and never come back.

SIBYL (*aghast*). What? But I don't understand. Why, Mummy? (MRS. RAILTON-BELL *does not reply.*) Mummy, tell me, why?

MRS. RAILTON-BELL. I can't tell you, dear. It might upset you too much.

SIBYL. But I must know, Mummy. I must. What has he done?

MRS. RAILTON-BELL (*after only the slightest hesitation*). You really *insist* I should tell you?

SIBYL. Yes, I do.

MRS. RAILTON-BELL. Even after my strong warning?

SIBYL. Yes.

MRS. RAILTON-BELL (*with a sigh*). Very well, then, dear.
I have no option, I suppose.

With a quick gesture she hands the paper to SIBYL.

Read that. Middle column. Half-way down. Ex-officer bound
over.

SIBYL *reads*. MRS. RAILTON-BELL *watches her. Suddenly*
SIBYL *sits, her eyes staring, but her face blank.* LADY
MATHESON *comes in. She sees* SIBYL *instantly.*

LADY MATHESON (*shocked*). Oh, Maud, you haven't –

MRS. RAILTON-BELL. I did my best, my dear, but she
insisted. She absolutely insisted. (*Solicitously bending over
her daughter's chair.*) I'm so sorry, my dear. It must be the
most dreadful shock for you. It was for us too, as you can
imagine. Are you all right?

SIBYL *takes her spectacles off and folding the paper
meticulously, lays it down on the arm of her chair. She makes
no reply.*

(*Slightly more sharply.*) Are you all right, Sibyl?

SIBYL (*barely audible*). Yes, Mummy.

JEAN *comes in, looking rather annoyed.*

JEAN. What is it, Mrs. Railton-Bell? I can only stay a moment.
I must get back to the baby.

MRS. RAILTON-BELL. I won't keep you long, I promise you.
Take a seat. (*Turning to* SIBYL, *sharply.*) Sibyl, what have
you done?

CHARLES *comes in.*

(*She takes* SIBYL's *glasses from her hand.*) Look, you've
broken your glasses.

SIBYL (*murmuring*). How stupid.

CHARLES. Hullo, you've cut your hand, haven't you?

SIBYL. No.

CHARLES. Yes, you have. Let's see.

With a rather professional air he picks up her limp hand and examines it.

Nothing much. No splinters. Here, you'd better have this. It's quite clean.

He takes a clean handkerchief from his breast pocket and ties it neatly round her hand.

Iodine and a bit of plaster later.

MR. FOWLER *has come in.*

MRS. RAILTON-BELL. Ah, Mr. Fowler, good. Would you take a seat, and then we can begin. The two young people are in a hurry. I'm afraid I have very grave news for you all.

CHARLES. The boiler's gone wrong again?

MRS. RAILTON-BELL. No. I only wish it were something so trivial.

CHARLES. I don't consider shaving in cold, brown water trivial.

MRS. RAILTON-BELL. Please, Mr. Stratton.

MR. FOWLER (*anxiously*). They're raising the prices again?

MRS. RAILTON-BELL. No. My news is graver even than that.

MR. FOWLER. I don't know what could be graver than that.

MRS. RAILTON-BELL. The news I have to give you, Mr Fowler.

CHARLES. Look, Mrs. Railton-Bell, must we play twenty questions? Can't you just tell us what it is?

MRS. RAILTON-BELL (*angrily*). My hesitation is only because the matter is so painful and so embarrassing for me that I find it difficult to choose my words. However, if you want it baldly, you shall have it. (*After a dramatic pause.*) Major Pollock – who is not a major at all but a lieutenant promoted from the ranks in the R.A.S.C. –

CHARLES (*excitedly*). No. You don't say! I knew it, you know. I always knew Sandhurst and the Black Watch was a phoney. Didn't I say so, Jean?

JEAN. Yes, you did, but I said it first – that night he made the boob about serviettes.

MR. FOWLER (*chipping in quickly*). I must admit I've always slightly suspected the public-school education, I mean only today he made the most shocking mistake in quoting Horace – quite appalling.

MRS. RAILTON-BELL (*raising her voice*). Please, please. ladies and gentlemen. This is not the point. The dreadful, the really ghastly revelation is still to come.

She gains silence, and once again pauses dramatically.

He was found guilty –

LADY MATHESON. Pleaded guilty –

MRS. RAILTON-BELL. Please. Gladys. He was found or pleaded guilty – I don't really see that it matters which – to behaving insultingly to no less than six respectable women in a Bournemouth cinema.

There is an aghast silence.

CHARLES (*at length*). Good God! What a performance.

LADY MATHESON. Really, Maud, I must correct that. I must. We only know one was respectable – the one who complained – and even she seemed a little odd in her behaviour. Why didn't she just say straight out to the Major: 'I do wish you'd stop doing whatever it is that you are, doing'? That's what I'd have done. About the other five we don't know anything at all. We don't even know if he nudged them or anything.

MRS. RAILTON-BELL. Of course he nudged them. He was in that cinema for an immoral purpose – he admitted it. And he was seen to change his seat five times – always choosing one next to female persons.

CHARLES. That could make ten nudges, really, couldn't it? If he had the chance of using both elbows?

JEAN. Eleven, with the original one. Or twelve, supposing –

MRS. RAILTON-BELL. Really, we seem to be losing the essential point in a welter of trivialities. The point is surely that the Major – the so-called Major – has pleaded guilty to a criminal offence of a disgusting nature, and I want to know what action we regular residents propose to take.

MR. FOWLER. What action do you propose, Mrs. Railton-Bell?

MRS. RAILTON-BELL. I propose, on your behalf, to go to Miss Cooper and demand that he leaves the hotel forthwith.

CHARLES. No.

MRS. RAILTON-BELL. You disagree, Mr. Stratton?

CHARLES. Yes, I do. Please don't think I'm making light of this business, Mrs. Railton-Bell. To me what he's done, if he's done it, seems ugly and repulsive. I've always had an intense dislike of the more furtive forms of sexual expression. So emotionally I'm entirely on your side. But logically I'm not.

MRS. RAILTON-BELL (*cuttingly*). Are you making a speech, Mr. Stratton? If so, perhaps you'd like to stand over there and address us.

CHARLES. No. I'm all right where I am, thank you. I'm not making a speech either. I'm just saying that my dislike of the Major's offence is emotional and not logical. My lack of understanding of it is probably a shortcoming in me. The Major presumably understands my form of lovemaking. I *should* therefore understand his. But I don't. So I am plainly in a state of prejudice against him, and must be very wary of any moral judgments I may pass in this matter. It's only fair to approach it from the purely logical standpoint of practical Christian ethics, and ask myself the question: 'What harm has the man done?' Well, apart from possibly slightly bruising the arm of a certain lady, whose motives in complaining – I agree with Lady Matheson – are extremely questionable – apart from that, and apart from telling us a few rather pathetic lies about his past life, which most of us do anyway from time to time, I really can't see he's done anything to justify us chucking him out into the street.

JEAN (*hotly*). I don't agree at all. I feel disgusted at what he's done too, but *I* think I'm quite right to feel disgusted. I don't consider myself prejudiced at all, and I think that people who behave like that are a public menace and deserve anything they get.

CHARLES. Your vehemence is highly suspect. I must have you psycho-analysed.

JEAN. It's absolutely logical, Charles. Supposing next time it's a daughter –

CHARLES (*wearily*). I know. I know. And supposing in twenty or thirty years' time she sits next to a Major Pollock in a cinema –

JEAN. Exactly. (*He laughs.*) It's not funny, Charles. How would you feel –

CHARLES. Very ashamed of her if she didn't use her elbows back, very hard, and in the right place.

JEAN. Charles, I think that's an absolutely monstrous –

MRS. RAILTON-BELL. Please, please, please. This is not a private argument between the two of you. I take it, Mr. Stratton, you are against any action regarding this matter? (CHARLES *nods*.) Of any kind at all?

CHARLES *shakes his head*.

Not even a protest?

CHARLES. I might give him a reproving glance at dinner.

MRS. RAILTON-BELL (*turning from him in disgust*). You, Mrs. Stratton, I gather, agree with me that I should see Miss Cooper.

JEAN (*firmly*.) Yes.

CHARLES (*murmuring to her.*) Book-burner.

JEAN (*furiously*.) What's book-burning got to do with it?

CHARLES. A lot.

MRS. RAILTON-BELL (*imperiously*). Quiet please. (*Turning to* MR. FOWLER.) Mr. Fowler? What do you think?

MR. FOWLER (*confused*). Well, it's difficult. Very difficult. I can't say I see it like Stratton. That's the modern viewpoint, I know – nothing is really wrong that doesn't do actual and accessible harm to another human being. But he's not correct when he calls that Christianity. Christianity, surely, goes much further than that. Certain acts are wrong because they are, in themselves and by themselves, impure and immoral, and it seems to me that this terrible wave of vice and sexual excess which seems to have flooded this country since the war might well, in part, be due to the decline of the old standards, emotional and illogical though they may well seem to the younger generation. Tolerance is not necessarily a good, you know. Tolerance of evil may itself be an evil. After all it was Aristotle, wasn't it, who said –

MISS MEACHAM *appears from the garden.*

MISS MEACHAM. Oh really – you've all gone on far too long about it. And when you start quoting Aristotle, well, personally, I'm going to my room.

MRS. RAILTON-BELL. You heard, Miss Meacham?

MISS MEACHAM. I couldn't help hearing. I didn't want to. I was doing my system and you need to concentrate like billy-oh on that, but I had my chair against the wall to catch the sun, and I wasn't going to move into the cold just for you people.

MRS. RAILTON-BELL. Well, as you know the facts, I suppose we should canvass your opinion. What is it?

MISS MEACHAM. I haven't any.

MRS. RAILTON-BELL. You must have *some* opinion?

MISS MEACHAM. Why should I? I've been out of the world for far longer than any of you and what do I know about morals and ethics? Only what I read in novels, and as I only read thrillers, that isn't worth much. In Peter Cheyney the hero does far worse things to his girls than the Major's done, and no one seems to mind.

MRS. RAILTON-BELL. I don't think that it's quite the point what Peter Cheyney's heroes do to his girls, Miss Meacham. We want your views on Major Pollock.

MISS MEACHAM. Do you? Well, my views on Major Pollock have always been that he's a crashing old bore, and a wicked old fraud. Now I hear he's a dirty old man, too, well, I'm not at all surprised, and quite between these four walls, I don't give a damn.

She goes out. There is a pause, and then MRS. RAILTON-BELL *turns to* MR. FOWLER.

MRS. RAILTON-BELL. Well, Mr. Fowler, I take it you are on the side of action?

Pause.

MR. FOWLER. I once had to recommend a boy for expulsion. Only once, in the whole of the fifteen years I was a housemaster. I was deeply unhappy about it. Deeply. And yet events proved me right. He was no good. He became a thief and a blackmailer, and – oh – horrible things happened to him. Horrible. (*After a moment's pause.*) Poor boy. He *had* a way with him –

MRS. RAILTON-BELL (*impatiently*). Are you in favour of action, Mr. Fowler?

MR. FOWLER (*unhappily*). Yes, I suppose so. Yes, I am.

MRS. RAILTON-BELL (*to* LADY MATHESON). And you, Gladys?

As LADY MATHESON *hesitates.*

You don't need to make a speech like the others, dear. Just say yes or no.

Pause.

LADY MATHESON (*at length*). Oh dear!

MRS. RAILTON-BELL. Now don't shilly-shally, Gladys. You know perfectly well what you feel about all this dreadful vice that's going on all over the country. You've told me often how people like that should be locked up –

LADY MATHESON (*at length*). Oh dear!

MRS. RAILTON-BELL (*really impatient*). Oh, for heaven's sake, make up your mind, Gladys. Are you on the side of Mr. Stratton with his defence of vice, or are you on the side of the Christian virtues like Mr. Fowler, Mrs. Stratton and myself?

CHARLES (*quietly*). I have never in my life heard a question more disgracefully begged. Senator McCarthy could use your talents, Mrs. Railton-Bell.

MRS. RAILTON-BELL. Will you keep quiet! Well, Gladys. which is it to be?

LADY MATHESON. I'm on your side, of course. It's only –

MRS. RAILTON-BELL (*to* CHARLES). Well, Mr. Stratton – apart from Miss Meacham, who might be said to be neutral, the count appears now to be five to one against you.

CHARLES. *Five* to one?

MRS. RAILTON-BELL. My daughter, of course, agrees with me.

CHARLES. How do you know?

MRS. RAILTON-BELL. I know her feelings in this matter.

CHARLES. May we hear them from herself?

SIBYL, *during the whole of this discussion, has not stirred in her chair. Her two hands, one bound with a handkerchief, have rested motionless in her lap, and she has been staring at the wall opposite her.*

Miss Railton-Bell – could we hear your views?

There is no reply.

MRS. RAILTON-BELL. Mr. Stratton is asking you a question, dear.

SIBYL. Yes, Mummy?

CHARLES. Could we hear your views?

SIBYL. My views?

MRS. RAILTON-BELL (*clearly, as to a child*). On Major
Pollock, dear. What action should we take about him?

SIBYL *seems puzzled and makes no reply.*

(*To the others, in an aside.*) It's the shock. (*To* SIBYL *again.*)
You know what you've just read in that paper, dear? What do
you think of it?

SIBYL (*in a whisper*). It made me sick.

MRS. RAILTON-BELL. Of course it did, dear. That's how we
all feel.

SIBYL (*her voice growing louder in a crescendo*). It made me.
sick. It made me sick. It made me sick. It made me sick.

MRS. RAILTON-BELL (*going quickly to her and embracing
her*). Yes, dear. Yes. Don't fuss now, don't fuss. It's all right.

SIBYL (*burying her face in her mother's arms*). I don't feel
well, Mummy. Can I go and lie down?

MRS. RAILTON-BELL. Of course you can, dear. We can go
into the writing-room. Such a nice comfy sofa, and there's
never anyone there. (*She leads her to the hall door.*) And
don't fret any more, my dear. Try and forget the whole nasty
business. Make believe it never happened – that there never
was such a person as Major Pollock. That's the way.

They disappear together into the hall.

LADY MATHESON. She should never have told her like that.
It was such a mistake.

CHARLES (*angrily*). I agree. If that girl doesn't end as a mental
case it won't be the fault of her mother.

LADY MATHESON (*loyally*). Mr. Stratton – I must say I
consider that a quite outrageous way of twisting my remark.
I used the word 'mistake', and you have no right –

CHARLES. No, I haven't. I'm sorry. The comment was purely my own.

JEAN. It was *your* fault for asking her views,

CHARLES. She was sitting there quite peacefully, apparently listening. I wasn't to know she was in a state of high suppressed hysteria. I might, admittedly, have guessed, but anyway, I had an idiotic but well-meaning hope that I might get her – just this once – just this once in the whole of her life-to disagree publicly with her mother. It could save her soul if she ever did. –

MR. FOWLER. I didn't realize that modern psychiatry recognized so old-fashioned and sentimental a term as soul, Mr. Stratton.

CHARLES. Very well, for soul read mind, and one day when you have a spare ten minutes explain to me the difference.

MR. FOWLER. I will.

CHARLES (*getting up*). Not now, I'm afraid. It might muddle my anatomical studies. (*To* JEAN.) Are you coming?

JEAN *gets up, rather reluctantly.*

JEAN. I don't know what's the matter with you, this evening, Charles. You're behaving like an arrogant pompous boor.

CHARLES. You must forgive me. I suppose it's just that I'm feeling a little light-headed at finding myself, on an issue of common humanity, in a minority of one. The sin of spiritual pride, that's called – isn't it, Mr. Fowler?

He goes out. JEAN *comes back from the door.*

JEAN (*to the other two*). He's been overworking, you know. He'll be quite different about all this tomorrow. (*Confidently.*) I'll see to that.

MRS. RAILTON-BELL *comes in.*

MRS. RAILTON-BELL. She's quite all right, now. She always recovers from these little states very quickly. She's resting in the writing-room.

LADY MATHESON. Oh good.

JEAN. I was just apologizing for my husband's behaviour, Mrs. Railton-Bell.

MRS. RAILTON-BELL. Thank you, my dear – but what I always say is – we're all of us entitled to our own opinions, however odd and dangerous and distasteful they may sometimes be. (*Briskly.*) Now. Shall we all go and see Miss Cooper in a body, or would you rather I acted as your spokesman?

It is plain which course she would prefer. After a pause, they begin to murmur diffidently.

LADY MATHESON. I think, perhaps, if *you* went, dear –

MR. FOWLER. I don't think a deputation is a good idea –

JEAN. You be our spokesman.

MRS. RAILTON-BELL. Very well.

She picks up the copy of the newspaper and goes to the door.

I hope you all understand it's a duty I hardly relish.

She goes out.

MR. FOWLER (*to* LADY MATHESON). I would hardly call that a strictly accurate self-appraisal, would you?

LADY MATHESON (*doubtfully*). Well – after all – doing a duty can seem a pleasure, to some people, can't it? It never has done to me, I agree, but then I'm – well – so weak and silly about these things –

JEAN (*at the door*). It would be a pleasure to me in this case. Horrid old man! (*To herself as she goes.*) I hope the baby's not been crying –

She goes out.

MR. FOWLER. A ruthless young girl, that, I would say.

LADY MATHESON. So many young people are these days, don't you think?

MR. FOWLER (*meaningly*). Not only young people.

LADY MATHESON (*unhappily*). Yes – well. (*With a sigh.*) Oh dear! What a dreadful affair. It's made me quite miserable.

MR. FOWLER. I feel a little unhappy about it all myself. (*He sighs and gets up.*) The trouble about being on the side of right, as one sees it, is that one sometimes finds oneself in the company of such very questionable allies. Let's go and take our minds off it all with television.

LADY MATHESON (*getting up*). Yes. Good idea. The news-reel will be nearly over now – but I think that dear Philip Harben is on, after. Such a pity I'll never have the chance of following any of his recipes.

MR. FOWLER (*as they go out*). I agree. One suffers the tortures of Tantalus, and yet the pleasure is intense. Isn't that what is today called masochism?

They go out. The room is empty for a moment, and then MAJOR POLLOCK *tentatively appears at the open french windows. He peers cautiously into the room, and, satisfying himself that it is empty, comes in. He goes quickly to the table on which are* MRS. RAILTON-BELL's *journals. He sees at once that the 'West Hampshire Weekly News' is no longer where he left it. Frantically he rummages through the pile, and then begins to search the room. He is standing, in doubt, by the fireplace, when the door opens quietly and* SIBYL *comes in. As she sees him she stands stock still. He does not move either.*

MAJOR POLLOCK (*at length, with pathetic jauntiness*). Evening, Miss R.B. And how's the world with you, eh?

SIBYL. Were you looking for Mummy's paper?

MAJOR POLLOCK. What? No, of course not. I've got the other copy –

SIBYL. Don't pretend any more, please. She's read it, you see.

MAJOR POLLOCK. Oh.

There is a long pause. The MAJOR*'s shoulders droop, and he holds the table for support.*

MAJOR POLLOCK. Did she show it to you?

SIBYL. Yes.

MAJOR POLLOCK. Oh.

SIBYL. And to all the others.

MAJOR POLLOCK. Miss Cooper too?

SIBYL. Mummy's gone to tell her.

The MAJOR *nods, hopelessly.*

MAJOR POLLOCK (*at length*). Well – that's it, then, isn't it?

SIBYL. Yes.

MAJOR POLLOCK. Oh God!

He sits down, staring at the floor. She looks at him steadily.

SIBYL (*passionately*). Why did you do it? Why did you do it?

MAJOR POLLOCK. I don't know. I wish I could answer that. Why does anyone do anything they shouldn't? Why do some people drink too much, and other people smoke fifty cigarettes a day? Because they can't stop it, I suppose.

SIBYL. Then this wasn't – the first time?

MAJOR POLLOCK (*quietly*). No.

SIBYL. It's horrible.

MAJOR POLLOCK. Yes, Of course it is. I'm not trying to defend it. You wouldn't guess, I know. but ever since school I've always been scared to death of women. Of everyone, in a way, I suppose, but mostly of women. I had a bad time at school – which wasn't Wellington, of course – just a Council school. Boys hate other boys to be timid and shy, and they gave it to me good and proper. My father despised me, too, He was a sergeant-major in the Black Watch. He made me join the Army, but I was always a bitter disappointment to him. He died before I got my I commission. I only got that by a wangle. It wasn't difficult at the beginning of

the war. But it meant everything to me, all the same. Being
saluted, being called sir – I thought I'm someone, now, a real
person. Perhaps some woman might even – (*He stops.*) But
it didn't work. It never has worked. I'm made in a certain
way, and I can't change it. It has to be the dark, you see, and
strangers, because –

SIBYL (*holding her hands to her ears*). Stop, stop. I don't want
to hear it. It makes me ill.

MAJOR POLLOCK (*quietly*). Yes. It would, of course. I should
have known that. It was only that you'd asked me about why
I did such things, and I wanted to talk to someone about it. I
never have, you see, not in the whole of my life. (*He gets up
and gently touches her sleeve.*) I'm sorry to have upset *you*,
of all people.

He goes to a table and collects two books.

SIBYL. Why me, so especially? Why not the others?

MAJOR POLLOCK. Oh, I don't give a hang about the others.
They'll all take it in their various ways, I suppose – but it
won't mean much more to them than another bit of gossip to
snort or snigger about. But it'll be, different for you, Sibyl,
and that makes me unhappy.

SIBYL. That's the first time you've ever called me Sibyl.

MAJOR POLLOCK. Is it? Well, there's not much point in all
that Miss R.B. stuff now, is there?

SIBYL. What makes me so different from the others?

The MAJOR *has gathered another book from a corner of the
room, and a pipe. He turns now and looks at her.*

MAJOR POLLOCK. Your being so scared of – well – shall we
call it life? It sounds more respectable than the word which I
know you hate. You and I are awfully alike, you know.
That's why I suppose we've drifted so much together in this
place.

SIBYL. How can you say we're alike? *I* don't – (*She stops,
unable to continue.*)

MAJOR POLLOCK. I know you don't. You're not even tempted and never will be. You're very lucky. Or are you? Who's to say, really? All I meant was that we're both of us frightened of people, and yet we've somehow managed to forget our fright when we've been in each other's company. Speaking for myself, I'm grateful and always will be. Of course I can't expect *you* to feel the same way now.

SIBYL. What are you doing?

MAJOR POLLOCK. Getting my things together. Have you seen a pouch anywhere?

SIBYL. It's here.

She goes to a table and collects it. He takes it from her.

MAJOR POLLOCK (*with a wry smile*). Old Wellingtonian colours.

SIBYL. Why have you told so many awful lies?

MAJOR POLLOCK. I don't like myself as I am, I suppose, so I've had to invent another person. It's not so harmful, really. We've all got daydreams. Mine have gone a step further than most people's – that's all. Quite often I've even managed to believe in the Major myself. (*He starts.*) Is that someone in the hall?

SIBYL (*listening*). No. I don't think so. Where will you go?

MAJOR POLLOCK. I don't know. There's a chap in London might put me up for a day or two. Only I don't so awfully want to go there –

SIBYL. Why not?

MAJOR POLLOCK (*after a slight pause*). Well – you see – it's rather a case of birds of a feather.

SIBYL. Don't go to him. You mustn't go to him.

MAJOR POLLOCK. I don't know where else.

SIBYL. Another hotel.

MAJOR POLLOCK. It can't be Bournemouth or anywhere near here. It'll have to be London, and I don't know anywhere there I can afford –

SIBYL. I'll lend you some money.

MAJOR POLLOCK. You certainly won't.

SIBYL. I will. I have some savings certificates. You can have those. I can get more too, if you need it.

MAJOR POLLOCK (*holding her hand, gently*). No, Sybil. No. Thank you – but no.

SIBYL. But you'll go to this man.

MAJOR POLLOCK. No, I won't. I'll find somewhere else.

SIBYL. Where?

MAJOR POLLOCK. Don't worry. I'll be all right.

MISS COOPER *comes in, and closes the door behind her.*

MISS COOPER (*brightly*). There you are, Major Pollock. Can I see you in my office a moment?

MAJOR POLLOCK. We don't need to talk in your office, Miss Cooper. I know what you have to say. I'm leaving at once.

MISS COOPER. I see. That's your own choice, is it?

MAJOR POLLOCK. Of course.

MISS COOPER. Because I would like to make it perfectly plain to you that there's no question whatever of my requiring you to leave this hotel. If you want to stay on here you're at perfect liberty to do so. It's entirely a matter for you.

Pause.

MAJOR POLLOCK. I see. That's good of you. But of course, I have to go.

MISS COOPER. I quite understand that you'd want to. I shan't charge the usual week's notice. When will you be going? Before dinner?

MAJOR POLLOCK. Of course.

MISS COOPER. Do you want me to help you find some place to stay until you can get settled?

MAJOR POLLOCK. I can hardly expect that, Miss Cooper.

MISS COOPER. Why on earth not? There are two hotels in London run by the Beauregard group. One is in West Kensington and the other in St. John's Wood. They're both about the same price. Which would you prefer?

MAJOR POLLOCK (*after a pause*). West Kensington, I think.

MISS COOPER. I've got their card here somewhere. Yes, there's one here.

She goes to the mantelpiece and takes a card from a small holder. She hands it to him.

Would you like me to ring them up for you?

MAJOR POLLOCK. Thank you, but I think perhaps I'd better ring them myself. In case of – further trouble, I don't want to involve you more than I need. May I use the phone in your office?

MISS COOPER. Certainly.

MAJOR POLLOCK. I'll pay for the call of course.

He goes to the door and looks to see if anyone is about in the hall.

Sibyl, if I don't have a chance of seeing you again, I'll write and say good-bye.

He goes out. MISS COOPER *turns to* SIBYL.

MISS COOPER. Your mother's gone up to dress for dinner, Miss Railton-Bell. She told me I'd find you in the writing-room lying down and I was to tell you that you can have your meal upstairs tonight, if you'd rather.

SIBYL. That's all right.

MISS COOPER (*sympathetically*). How are you feeling now?

SIBYL (*brusquely*). All right.

MISS COOPER *approaches her.*

MISS COOPER (*quietly*). Is there anything I can do to help you?

SIBYL (*angrily*). No. Nothing. And please don't say things like that. You'll make me feel bad again, and I'll make a fool of myself. I feel well now. He's going and that's good. I despise him.

MISS COOPER. Do you? I wonder if you should.

SIBYL. He's a vile, wicked man, and he's done a horrible beastly thing. It's not the first time, either. He admits that.

MISS COOPER. I didn't think it was.

SIBYL. And yet you told him he could stay on in the hotel if he wanted to? That's wicked too.

MISS COOPER. Then I suppose I *am* wicked too. (*She puts her hand on her arm.*) Sibyl, dear –

SIBYL. Why is everyone calling me Sibyl this evening? Please stop. You'll only make me cry.

MISS COOPER. I don't mean to do that. I just mean to help you.

SIBYL *breaks down suddenly but now quietly and without hysteria.* MISS COOPER *holds her.*

That's better. Much better.

SIBYL. It's so horrible.

MISS COOPER. I know it is. I'm very sorry for you.

SIBYL. He says we're alike – he and I.

MISS COOPER. Does he?

SIBYL. He says we're both scared of life and people and sex. There – I've said the word. He says I hate *saying* it even, and he's right. I do. What's the matter with me? There must be something the matter with me.

MISS COOPER. Nothing very much, I should say. Shall we sit down?

She gently propels her on to the sofa and sits beside her.

SIBYL. I'm a freak, aren't I ?

MISS COOPER (*in matter-of-fact tones*). I never know what that word means. If you mean you're different from other people, then, I suppose, you are a freak. But all human beings are a bit different from each other, aren't they? What a dull world it would be if they weren't.

SIBYL. I'd like to be ordinary.

MISS COOPER. I wouldn't know about that. dear. You see, I've never met an ordinary person. To me all people are extraordinary. I meet all sorts here, you know, in my job, and the one thing I've learnt in five years is that the word normal, applied to any human being, is utterly meaningless. In a sort of a way it's an insult to our Maker, don't you think, to suppose that He could possibly work to any set pattern.

SIBYL. I don't think Mummy would agree with you.

MISS COOPER. I'm fairly sure she wouldn't. Tell me – when did your father die?

SIBYL. When I was seven.

MISS COOPER. Did you go to school?

SIBYL. No. Mummy said I was too delicate. I had a governess some of the time, but most of the time Mummy taught me herself.

MISS COOPER. Yes. I see. And you've never really been away from her, have you?

SIBYL. Only when I had a job, for a bit. (*Proudly.*) I was a sales-girl in a big shop in London – Jones & Jones. I sold lampshades. But I got ill, though, and had to leave.

MISS COOPER (*brightly*). What bad luck. Well, you must try again, some day, mustn't you?

SIBYL. Mummy says no.

MISS COOPER. Mummy says no. Well, then, you must just try and get Mummy to say yes, don't you think?

SIBYL. I don't know how.

MISS COOPER. I'll tell you how. By running off and getting a job on your own. She'll say yes quick enough then.

She pats SIBYL's *knee sympathetically and gets up.*

I have my menus to do. (*She goes towards the door.*)

SIBYL (*urgently*). Will he be all right, do you think?

MISS COOPER. The Major? I don't know. I hope so.

SIBYL. In spite of what he's done, I don't want anything bad to happen to him. I want him to be happy. Is it a nice hotel – this one in West Kensington ?

MISS COOPER. Very nice.

SIBYL. Do you think he'll find a friend there? He told me just now that he'd always be grateful to me for making him forget how frightened he was of people.

MISS COOPER. He's helped you too, hasn't he?

SIBYL. Yes.

MISS COOPER (*after a pause*). I hope he'll find a friend in the new hotel.

SIBYL. So do I. Oh God, so do I.

The MAJOR *comes in.*

MAJOR POLLOCK (*quickly, to* MISS COOPER). It's all right. I've fixed it. It might please you to know that I said *Mr.* Pollock, and didn't have to mention your name, or this hotel. I must dash upstairs and pack now.

He turns to SIBYL *and holds out his hand.*

Good-bye, Sybil.

SIBYL *takes his hand, after a second's hesitation.*

SIBYL. Good-bye.

She drops his hand and runs quickly to the door.

(*Without looking back.*) God bless you.

She goes out.

MAJOR POLLOCK. Very upset? (MISS COOPER *nods*.)
That's the part I've hated most, you know. It's funny. She's
rather an odd one – almost a case – she's got a child's mind
and hardly makes sense sometimes – and yet she means quite
a lot to me.

MISS COOPER. I think you mean quite a lot to her too.

MAJOR POLLOCK. I did, I think. Not now, of course. It was
the gallant ex-soldier she was fond of – not – (*He stops*.)
I told her the whole story about myself. I thought it right.
There's just a chance she might understand it all a bit better
one day. I'm afraid, though, she'll never get over it.

MISS COOPER. No. I don't suppose she will.

MAJOR POLLOCK. One's apt to excuse oneself sometimes by
saying: Well, after all, what I do doesn't do anybody much
harm. But one does, you see. That's not a thought I like.
Could you have a squint in the hall and see if anyone's
around?

MISS COOPER *half-opens the door.*

MISS COOPER. Miss Meacham's at the telephone.

MAJOR POLLOCK. Damn.

MISS COOPER. What train are you catching?

MAJOR POLLOCK. Seven forty-five.

MISS COOPER. You've got time.

MAJOR POLLOCK. I've got a tremendous lot of packing to
do. Four years, you know. Hellish business. I'm dreading the
first few days in a new place. I mean dreading, you know –
literally trembling with funk at the thought of meeting new
people. The trouble is I'll probably be forced by sheer terror
to take refuge in all that Major stuff again.

MISS COOPER. Try not to.

MAJOR POLLOCK. Oh, I'll try all right. I'll try. I only hope
I'll succeed.

He goes cautiously to the door and turns.

Still there. Damn. (*Coming back.*) Thank you for being so kind. God knows why you have been. I don't deserve it – but I'm grateful. Very grateful.

MISS COOPER. That's all right.

MAJOR POLLOCK. You're an odd fish, you know, if you don't mind my saying so. A good deal more goes on behind that calm managerial front of yours than anyone would imagine. Has something bad ever happened to you ?

MISS COOPER. Yes.

MAJOR POLLOCK. Very bad?

MISS COOPER. I've got over it.

MAJOR POLLOCK. What was it?

MISS COOPER. I loved a man who loved somebody else.

MAJOR POLLOCK. Still love him?

MISS COOPER. Oh yes. I always will.

MAJOR POLLOCK. Any hope?

MISS COOPER (*cheerfully*). No. None at all.

MAJOR POLLOCK. Why so cheerful about it?

MISS COOPER. Because there's no point in being anything else. I've settled for the situation, you see, and it's surprising how cheerful one can be when one gives up hope. I've still got the memory, you see, which is a very pleasant one – all things considered.

MAJOR POLLOCK (*nodding*). I see. Quite the philosopher, what? (*To himself.*) I must give up saying what. Well, Meacham or no Meacham, I'm going to make a dash for it. or I'll miss that train.

He turns back to the door.

MISS COOPER. Why don't you stay?

MAJOR POLLOCK (*turning, incredulously*). Stay? In the hotel, you mean?

MISS COOPER. You say you dread the new hotel.

MAJOR POLLOCK. I dread this one a damn sight more, now.

MISS COOPER. Yes, I expect you do. But at least you couldn't be forced by terror into any more Major stuff, could you?

Pause.

MAJOR POLLOCK. I might be forced into something a good deal more – conclusive – cleaning my old service revolver, perhaps – you know the form – make a nasty mess on one of your carpets and an ugly scandal in your hotel.

MISS COOPER (*lightly*). I'd take the risk, if you would.

MAJOR POLLOCK. My dear Miss Cooper, I'm far too much of a coward to stay on here now. Far too much.

MISS COOPER. I see. Pity. I just thought it would be so nice if you could prove to yourself that you weren't.

Pause.

MAJOR POLLOCK (*at length*). You're thinking of her too, of course, aren't you?

MISS COOPER. Yes.

MAJOR POLLOCK. Reinstate the gallant ex-soldier in her eyes?

MISS COOPER. That's right.

MAJOR POLLOCK. Make her think she's helped me find my soul and all that.

MISS COOPER. Yes.

Another pause.

MAJOR POLLOCK (*with an eventual sigh*). Not a hope. Not a hope in the whole, wide, blinking world. I know my form, you see.

MISS COOPER. I wonder if you do.

MAJOR POLLOCK (*sadly*). Oh I do. I do, only too well. Thanks for trying, anyway.

He looks cautiously out into the hall.

 Coast's clear.

He turns round and looks at her for a long time. She stares back steadily at him.

(*At length.*) There's a nine-something train, isn't there?

MISS COOPER. Nine thirty-two.

There is another pause as he looks at her in doubt. Then he gives a shamefaced smile.

MAJOR POLLOCK. I expect I'll still catch the seven forty-five.

He goes out.

The lights fade.

Scene Two

Scene: the dining-room. As at the beginning of the first play, dinner is in full swing. The table by the window is now occupied by a pair of young 'casuals' – much interested in each other, and totally oblivious of everyone else. One table is unoccupied and unlaid; otherwise all the tables are occupied by the usual owners.

As the lights come on, conversation is general – which means, more precisely, that the two casuals are murmuring together, the STRATTONS *are arguing,* LADY MATHESON *and* MR. FOWLER *are talking between tables, and* MRS. RAILTON-BELL *is talking to* SIBYL, MABEL *is hovering over* MISS MEACHAM *who is absorbed in 'Racing Up To Date'.*

MABEL (*heard above the background*). Were you the fricassee or the cambridge steak?

MISS MEACHAM. What? Oh, it doesn't matter. Both are uneatable.

MABEL. What about the cold chicken, then?

MISS MEACHAM. *Cold* chicken? But we haven't had it hot yet.

MABEL. If I were you I'd have the fricassee. It's all right. It's rabbit.

MISS MEACHAM. The fricassee then.

MR. FOWLER. Any cheese, Mabel?

MABEL. Afraid not.

MR. FOWLER. There's never any cheese.

MABEL *serves* MISS MEACHAM *and stumps out to the kitchen.* MRS. RAILTON-BELL *leans across to* LADY MATHESON.

MRS. RAILTON-BELL. I believe there's a new game on television tonight.

LADY MATHESON. Yes, I know, dear, I read all about it in the *Radio Times*. It sounds quite fascinating – I shall certainly see it next week.

MRS. RAILTON-BELL. Why not tonight, dear?

LADY MATHESON. I feel too tired. I'm going to go to bed directly after dinner.

MRS. RAILTON-BELL. Of course. (*Lowering her voice*.) What a really nerve-racking day it's been, hasn't it? I don't suppose any of us will ever forget it. Ever. I feel utterly shattered, myself. (*To* SIBYL.) Pass the sauce, dear.

LADY MATHESON nods. MRS. RAILTON-BELL takes a sip of wine.

The MAJOR *has walked quietly into the dining-room.* MRS. RAILTON-BELL *turns and stares unbelievingly at him as he walks slowly to his table and sits down. The conversation in the dining-room has frozen into a dead silence, for even the casuals seem affected by the electric atmosphere – though oblivious of the cause – and have ceased talking. The silence is broken by* DOREEN *entering the dining-room and seeing him.*

DOREEN (*calling through the kitchen door*). Mabel – Number Seven's in. You said he was out.

MABEL (*off*). Well, that's what Joe said. Joe said he was leaving before dinner.

DOREEN. Sorry, Major. There's been a muddle. I'll lay your table right away.

She goes back into the kitchen. The silence remains unbroken, until DOREEN *returns with a tray and begins quickly to lay the* MAJOR's *table.*

What would you like? The fricassee's nice.

MAJOR POLLOCK. I'll have that. Thank you.

DOREEN. Soup first?

MAJOR POLLOCK. No, thank you.

DOREEN (*finally laying the table*). There we are. All cosy now. Fricassee you said?

MAJOR POLLOCK. That's right.

She goes into the kitchen. SIBYL is staring at the MAJOR, but he does not meet her eyes. He is looking down at his table, as is everyone else, aware of his presence, save SIBYL and MRS. RAILTON-BELL who is glaring furiously in turn at him and at the others. The silence is broken suddenly by a rather nervously high-pitched greeting from CHARLES.

CHARLES (*to the* MAJOR). Hullo.

MAJOR POLLOCK (*murmuring*). Hullo.

CHARLES. Clouding over a bit, isn't it? I'm afraid we may get rain later.

JEAN is furiously glaring at her husband. MRS. RAILTON-BELL has turned fully round in her chair in an attempt to paralyse him into silence.

MAJOR POLLOCK. Yes. I'm afraid we may.

MISS MEACHAM. We need it. This hard going's murder on form. (*To* MAJOR POLLOCK.) You know Newmarket, don't you?

MAJOR POLLOCK. No, I don't.

MISS MEACHAM. But I remember your saying – (*She gets it.*) Oh, I see. Well, it's a very tricky course in hard going. Still, if they get some rain up there tomorrow, I think I'll be able to give you a winner on Tuesday.

MAJOR POLLOCK. Thank you. Thank you very much. The only thing is, I may not be here on Tuesday.

MISS MEACHAM. Oh, really? All right. Leave me your address then and I'll wire it to you. I'll need the money for the wire, though.

MAJOR POLLOCK. Thank you. That's very kind of you.

MISS MEACHAM. You won't think it so kind of me, if it loses.

She goes back to her 'Racing Up To Date'.

MISS COOPER *comes in.*

MISS COOPER (*brightly*). Good evening, Mrs. Railton-Bell. Good evening, Lady Matheson. Good evening, Mr. Pollock.

The 'Mr.' is barely distinguishable from 'Major', and her voice is as brightly 'managerial' to him as to the others.

I hear they didn't lay your table tonight. I'm so sorry.

MAJOR POLLOCK. Quite all right.

MISS COOPER. I'd advise the fricassee, if I were you. It's really awfully nice.

MAJOR POLLOCK. I've ordered it.

MISS COOPER. Good, I'm so glad. (*She passes on.*) Good evening, Mr. and Mrs. Stratton. Everything all right? (*They nod and smile.*) Splendid.

She bows rather less warmly to 'the casuals' and goes out.

MRS. RAILTON-BELL *pretends to feel an imaginary draught.*

MRS. RAILTON-BELL (*to* LADY MATHESON). It's very cold in here suddenly, don't you think, dear?

LADY MATHESON *nods, nervously.*

I think I'll turn my chair round a bit, and get out of the draught.

She does so, turning her back neatly on the MAJOR. MR. FOWLER *gets up quietly from his table and walks to the door. To do this he has to pass the* MAJOR. *A step or so past him he hesitates and then looks back, nods and smiles.*

MR. FOWLER. Good evening.

MAJOR POLLOCK. Good evening.

MRS. RAILTON-BELL *has had to twist her head sharply round in order to allow her eyes to confirm this shameful betrayal.*

MR. FOWLER. Hampshire did pretty well today, did you see? Three hundred and eighty-odd for five.

MAJOR POLLOCK. Very good.

MR. FOWLER. I wish they had more bowling. Well –

He smiles vaguely and goes on into the lounge. There is an audible and outraged 'Well!' from MRS. RAILTON-BELL. Silence falls again. Suddenly and by an accident the MAJOR's and LADY MATHESON's eyes meet. Automatically she inclines her head and gives him a slight smile. He returns the salute.

LADY MATHESON (*to* MAJOR POLLOCK). Good evening.

MRS. RAILTON-BELL (*in a whisper*). Gladys!

LADY MATHESON, who has genuinely acted from instinct, looks startled. Then she apparently decides to be as well hanged for a sheep as a lamb.

LADY MATHESON (*suddenly very bold, and in a loud voice*). I advise the apple charlotte. It's very good.

MAJOR POLLOCK. Thank you. I'll have that.

She is instantly conscience-stricken at what she has done and hangs her head over her apple charlotte, eating feverishly. She refuses to look at MRS. RAILTON-BELL, who is staring at her with wide, unbelieving and furious eyes. MRS. RAILTON-BELL, getting no response from LADY MATHESON, deliberately folds her napkin and rises.

MRS. RAILTON-BELL (*quietly*). Come, Sibyl.

SIBYL (*equally quietly*). I haven't finished yet, Mummy.

MRS. RAILTON-BELL (*looking puzzled at this unaccustomed response*). It doesn't matter, dear. Come into the lounge.

SIBYL makes no move to rise. She stares up at her mother.

There is a pause.

SIBYL. No, Mummy.

Pause.

MRS. RAILTON-BELL (*sharply*). Sibyl, come with me at once –

SIBYL (*with quiet firmness*). No, Mummy. I'm going to stay in the dining-room, and finish my dinner.

MRS. RAILTON-BELL *hesitates, plainly meditating various courses of action. Finally she decides on the only really possible course left to her – the dignified exit. Before she has got to the door* SIBYL *has spoken to the* MAJOR.

There's a new moon tonight, you know. We must all go and look at it afterwards.

MAJOR POLLOCK. Yes. We must.

DOREEN *has bustled in with the* MAJOR's *dish as* MRS. RAILTON-BELL, *her world crumbling, goes into the lounge.* DOREEN *serves* MAJOR POLLOCK.

DOREEN. Sorry it's been so long. You're a bit late, you see.

MAJOR POLLOCK. Yes. My fault.

DOREEN. What's the matter with you tonight? You always say 'mea culpa'.

She beats her breast in imitation of an obvious MAJOR *bon mot.*

MAJOR POLLOCK. Do I? Well – they both mean the same, don't they?

DOREEN. I suppose so. (*Finishing the serving.*) There you are. Now what about breakfast?

MAJOR POLLOCK. Breakfast?

DOREEN. Joe got it wrong about your going, didn't he?

There is a pause. SIBYL *is looking steadily at the* MAJOR, *who now raises his eyes from his plate and meets her glance.*

MAJOR POLLOCK (*quietly, at length*). Yes, he did.

DOREEN. That's good. Breakfast usual time, then?

MAJOR POLLOCK. Yes, Doreen. Breakfast usual time.

DOREEN *goes into the kitchen.* MAJOR POLLOCK *begins to eat his fricassee.* SIBYL *continues to eat her sweet. A decorous silence, broken only by the renewed murmur of 'the casuals', reigns once more, and the dining-room of the Beauregard Private Hotel no longer gives any sign of the battle that has just been fought and won between its four bare walls.*

Curtain.

Textual Variants

*For the American premiere, Rattigan wrote a series of alter-
native passages, altering the nature of Pollock's crime. They
were not used, and this is the first time they have been published
in their entirety. They replace those sections indicated by
marginal rules in the foregoing text.*

Page 78–79

MRS. RAILTON-BELL. No, no. Ex-officer bound over.

LADY MATHESON (*brightly*). Oh yes. (*Reading*.) 'Ex-officer
bound over. One a.m. arrest on Esplanade . . . ' (*Looking
up*.) On Esplanade? Oh dear – do we really want to hear
this?

MRS. RAILTON-BELL (*grimly*). Yes, we do. Go on.

LADY MATHESON (*reading resignedly*). 'On Thursday last,
before the Bournemouth magistrates, David Angus Pollock,
55, giving his address – ' (*She starts violently*.) ' – as the
Beauregard Hotel, Morgan Crescent – ' (*In a feverish
whisper*.) Major Pollock? Oh!

MRS. RAILTON-BELL. Go on.

LADY MATHESON (*reading*). ' Morgan Crescent – pleaded
guilty to a charge of persistently importuning – ' (*Her voice
sinks to a horrified murmur*.) 'male persons – ' (*She stops,
unable to go on. At length*.) Oh no. Oh no. He must have
been drinking.

MRS. RAILTON-BELL. He's a teetotaller.

LADY MATHESON. Perhaps just that one night.

MRS. RAILTON-BELL. No. Read on.

LADY MATHESON. 'A Mr. William Osborne, 38, of
4, Studland Row, giving evidence, said that at about eleven
fifteen p.m. on July the eighteenth Pollock had approached
him on the Esplanade, and had asked him for a light. He had
obliged and Pollock thereupon offered him a cigarette which
he accepted. A few words were exchanged following which
Pollock made a certain suggestion. He (Mr. Osborne) walked
away and issued a complaint to the first policeman he saw.
Under cross-examination by L.F. Crowther, the defendant's
counsel, Mr. Osborne admitted that he had twice previously
given evidence in Bournemouth in similar cases, but refused
to admit that he had acted as 'a stooge' for the police.
Counsel then observed that it was indeed a remarkable
coincidence. Inspector Franklin, giving evidence, said that
following Mr. Osborne's complaint a watch was kept on
Pollock for roughly an hour. During this time he was seen to
approach no less than four persons, on each occasion with an
unlighted cigarette in his mouth. There was quite a heavy
drizzle that night and the Inspector noted that on at least two
occasions the cigarette would not light, and Pollock had had
to throw it away. None of them, he admitted, had seemed
particularly disturbed or shocked by what was said to them
by the defendant, but of course this was not unusual in cases
of this kind. At one a.m. Pollock was arrested and, after
being charged and cautioned, stated: "You have made a
terrible mistake. You have the wrong man. I was only
walking home and wanted a light for my cigarette, I am a
Colonel in the Scots' Guards." Later he made a statement. A
petrol lighter, in perfect working order, was found in his
pocket. Mr. Crowther, in his plea for the defendant, stated
that his client had had a momentary aberration. He was
extremely sorry and ashamed of himself and would
undertake never to behave in so stupid and improper a
manner in future. He asked that his client's blameless record
should be taken into account. He had enlisted in the army in
1925 and in 1939 was granted a commission as a second
lieutenant in the Royal Army Service Corps.'

Page 80

LADY MATHESON. No, of course, it wouldn't have been better. One has to know these things, I suppose – although sometimes I wonder why.

MRS. RAILTON-BELL. Because if there's a liar and a fraudulent crook and a sexual pervert wandering around among us unsuspected, there could be well – there could be the most terrible repercussions.

LADY MATHESON. Well, he's been wandering around among us for four years now and there haven't been any repercussions yet. Oh heavens! –

MRS. RAILTON-BELL. What's the matter?

LADY MATHESON. I was thinking of poor Sibyl. Oh dear. And she's such a friend of his, isn't she? Oh dear, oh dear.

MRS. RAILTON-BELL. Exactly.

LADY MATHESON (*after a moment's troubled reflection*). Maud, dear – it's not my business, I know, and of course you have a mother's duty to protect your child, but of course, I do see – and yet – well she's such a strange girl – so excitable and shy – and so ungrownup in so many ways –

MRS. RAILTON-BELL. Come to the point, Gladys.

LADY MATHESON. Yes, I will. It's this. I don't think you ought to tell her this.

MRS. RAILTON-BELL. Not *tell* her?

LADY MATHESON. Well, not all of it. Not the details. Say he's a fraud, if you like, but not – please, Maud – not about the cigarettes. (*Suddenly distressed by the thought herself.*) Oh dear! I don't know how I shall ever look him in the face again.

Pages 85–86

LADY MATHESON. Pleaded guilty –

MRS. RAILTON-BELL. Please, Gladys. He was found or
pleaded guilty – I really don't see that it matters which –
to persistently importuning male persons on the Esplanade
between eleven fifteen p.m. and one a.m. on the night of July
the eighteenth, in that he made improper suggestions to no
less than four persons whom he asked for a light, no, five,
with the one who complained, and it was so wet that night
that on at least two occasions his cigarette just wouldn't light
at all, and he had to throw it away.

There is a pause.

CHARLES (*at length*). Well, at least he stood by the Guards'
slogan. Never admit defeat.

LADY MATHESON. Really, Maud, I must correct that. I must.
We don't know anything of what he said to these people.
Even the policeman admitted they didn't seem shocked, so
why shouldn't he just have been talking to them about the
weather?

MRS. RAILTON-BELL. What about the one who complained.

LADY MATHESON. He might easily have made a mistake
about the whole thing. I'm sure that's quite easy. I remember
once, in a bus, long ago, a man suddenly spoke to me and I
thought – well, anyway I'd *met* him at the Forsyths, and
clean forgotten, you see. Anyway I think this man Osborne
was very odd in his behaviour. Why on earth didn't he just
say straight out to the Major 'No thank you very much – but
I'm not like that – ' well perhaps not thank you very much,
but whatever it is in a case like that you do say – and then just
have gone on his way like the others instead of hanging
around in the rain and complaining. The others didn't
complain, after all.

MRS. RAILTON-BELL (*patiently*). He asked them all for a
light, dear, and a petrol lighter – in perfect working order –
was found in his pocket –

CHARLES. A petrol lighter is never in perfect working order. He should have had one of those gas things –

JEAN. You're just idiotic about those gas lighters, Charles. They're extremely expensive and they don't work any better than petrol –

MRS. RAILTON-BELL. Please, please. We seem to be losing the essential point in a welter of trivialities. The point is surely that the Major – the so-called Major – has pleaded guilty to a criminal offence of a disgusting nature, and I want to know what action we regular residents propose to take.

Page 86–87

CHARLES [*continuing present speech*] . . . It's only fair to approach it from the purely logical standpoint of practical Christian ethics, and ask myself the question: 'What harm has the man done?' Well, apart from apparently wounding the delicate susceptibilities of a Mr. Osborne – whose motives in complaining – I agree with Lady Matheson, are extremely suspect – apart from that, and apart from telling us a few rather pathetic lies about his past life, which most of us do anyway from time to time, I really can't see he's done anything to justify us chucking him out into the street.

JEAN (*hotly*). I don't agree at all. I feel disgusted at what he's done too, but *I* think I'm quite right to feel disgusted. I don't consider myself prejudiced at all, and I think that people who behave like that are a public menace and deserve anything they get.

CHARLES. Your vehemence is highly suspect. I must have you psycho-analysed.

JEAN. It's absolutely logical, Charles. Supposing your son –

CHARLES. I know. I know. Supposing in twenty or thirty years' time some Major Pollock on an esplanade asks *him* for a light –

JEAN. Exactly (*He laughs*.) It's not funny, Charles. How would *you* feel –

CHARLES. I hope he'd give him one and hop it. If he doesn't it'll be his look out.

JEAN. Charles, I think that's absolutely monstrous [–]

Pages 88–89

MISS MEACHAM. Why should I? I've been out of the world for far longer than any of you and what do I know about morals and ethics? Only what I read in novels, and as I only read thrillers, that isn't worth much. In Peter Cheyney the hero does far worse things than the Major's done – and nobody seems to mind.

MRS. RAILTON-BELL. I hardly think it's the point what Peter Cheyney's heroes do, Miss Meacham. We want your views on Major Pollock.